aurora metro press

Founded in 1989 to publish and promote new writing, the company has specialised in new drama and fiction, winning recognition and awards from the industry.

European series
A Touch of the Dutch: plays by women ed. Cheryl Robson
ISBN 0-9515877-7-3   £9.95

Mediterranean Plays by women ed. Marion Baraitser
ISBN 0-9515877-3-0   £9.95

Other new drama
Six Plays by Black and Asian women ed. Kadija George
ISBN 0-9515877-2-2   £7.50

Seven Plays by women: female voices, fighting lives
ed. Cheryl Robson ISBN 0-9515877-1-4   £5.95

Forthcoming
Young Blood: plays for young performers
ed. Sally Goldsworthy ISBN 0-9515877-6-5   £9.95

New fiction
How Maxine Learned to Love her legs and other tales of
growing up ed. Sarah Le Fanu ISBN 0-9515877-4-9   £8.95

and
The Women Writers Handbook ISBN 0-9515877-0-6   £4.95

Cheryl Robson

A playwright and editor, she founded the Women's Theatre Workshop in London in 1986 and was Artistic Director until 1995, producing and developing new writing by women. She has also worked in television, lectured at Westminster University and taken an MA in Playwrighting Studies at Birmingham University. She is the series editor for Aurora's collections of European Plays by Women.

*

My interest in the Dutch began early - with my first boyfriend. We went round the world together, well half-way. He was travelling to Amsterdam, I was travelling to Southampton from Sydney, Australia. I have him forever being thrown into the swimming pool by King Neptune as we sailed across the equator, captured for posterity on my father's 16mm cine films. I kept a journal of my trip from Australasia to Europe via Tahiti, Panama, Nassau and New York, which was the beginning of becoming a writer. I was eleven years old.

A
TOUCH
OF THE
DUTCH

plays by women

aurora metro press

theater instituut nederland

We gratefully acknowledge financial assistance from the Nederland Theatre Institute and the Royal Netherlands Embassy.

CONTENTS

Foreword
by Cheryl Robson

This is the second in our European Series of Plays by Women. The plays in this collection were selected from a large and wide-ranging group of modern dramatic works by women from the Netherlands. My selection is idiosyncratic in that I've chosen strong, topical works by writers whose voices I felt, illuminate the lives of contemporary women everywhere.

In making this selection, many good plays and important writers have been excluded. The work of Annie M.G. Schmidt is a fine example of this, her plays *Loose Sand* and *A tear on the Eclair* are particularly worth mentioning for their humour and social insight and she was immensely popular for her TV, radio and musical plays. Mia Meijer's period play *Cecile* about a nineteenth century proto-feminist writer explores notions of male/female roles in society and the class divisions that occur when a wealthy woman has an affair with one of her servants. Yvonne Keuls' *Anybody and his brother* takes a realist approach to the problems of young homeless people staying in a hostel and Frouke Fokkema's *The Detour* is a non-naturalistic exploration of the myth of the writer. Marion Boyer, Astrid Roemer and Wanda Reisel are also working in a non-naturalistic vein and their work offers promising material for directors with an interest in allegory and symbolism.

The range of plays, poetry, journalism and novels undertaken by the selected writers, many of whom have won awards and had their work translated into several languages, demonstrates the growth and inventiveness of Dutch women's literature. In bringing these plays to you in new translations, I hope to connect English-speaking theatre practitioners with some of the best contemporary work available elsewhere in Europe.

Introduction
by Mieke Kolk
translated by Purni Morell

Five plays by Dutch writers, relative unknowns in the English-speaking world; one is from the late fifties, the others are more contemporary. What they have in common is a particular concern for their female characters, their possibilities and the choices open to them in their fictitious lives. What separates the four later plays from the earlier one is a changed perception of human identity. Character is no longer understood as a psychological unity but as a floating construct of different, culturally determined positions. The consequent divergence of perspectives often leads to a more fragmented and open-ended dramatic structure. This is a development shared by the drama of a number of European countries, most notably Germany, where Dutch plays are frequently performed.

The most celebrated of the five writers is the eldest, namely Hella Haasse (b. 1918). In the post-war years she wrote a number of impressive historical novels and, during the course of time, her work came to focus on literary biography based on authentic source material. Several of these books became best-sellers in Holland. Haasse's work has been translated into German, French, Italian and English.

A Thread in the Dark (De Draad in het donker) is the more frequently performed of her plays. Although she trained as an actress, marriage (as she puts it) left her little time to build her career in the theatre. As a reworking of a Greek myth, the play follows the predominantly French tradition of rewriting classical tragedy in the 1930's and 40's. Jean Giraudoux, Jean Anouilh and Marguerite Yourcenar all reworked tragedies from a modern existential point of view. Haasse's chosen theme is closely linked to an investigation of political power, the betrayal and demagogy of those who wield it, and its unquestioned acceptance by the Cretan people when prosperity blinds them. The Minotaur, the Cretan monster which demands human sacrifice each year, doesn't actually exist in Haasse's version - rather it is a myth fabricated by King Minos with which he imbues the lives of the Cretans and legitimises them as a 'chosen people'. When his daughter Ariadne discovers the lie, she not only saves the young Athenian prince Theseus from the labyrinth but also demands that the truth come to light. On the return voyage to Athens, Theseus takes over the lie, not wanting to give up his position as the hero who killed the beast. In the mounting argument between the two, during which their very betrothal comes under scrutiny, Ariadne defends her standards of truth and humanity like a second Antigone. In the end, it is her younger sister Phaedra who, conforming to the female stereotype, leads Theseus to leave Ariadne behind on the uninhabited Naxos.

Although Haasse's later work presents a number of strong-willed female characters, she dislikes her work being categorised as feminist. If, she argues, an inundation of feminine thought and feeling appears in literature, that's purely advantageous, not particularly for political reasons but simply because such work is a necessary exploration of 'people of a feminine sex.'

An equally nuanced standpoint is taken by the writer Judith Herzberg (b. 1934). Interviewed in 1989, she said: 'I don't want to lay down the law or state moral claims in my work; what I try to do is to make the audience experience the same confusion that I feel when I look at reality.' This starting-point, which reflects her poetic works, has an extraordinary consequence for her stage plays. Her characters do not speak in well-formed dialogue but in seemingly disconnected fragments of text which come to the characters spontaneously as the product of a process of thought and experience, rather like the tip of an iceberg. Characters aren't in control of what they say - language controls them, welling up within them. The contours of their lives become apparent only in the patchwork of their words, and their secrets always remain buried beneath this surface. Such a writing style demands an approach by the actor which concentrates more on feeling for a way through a piece rather than interpreting and comprehension, perhaps not unlike the works of Pinter. Although the subject of her work is often heart-rending, the surface remains light and casual. After some delay, the audience will gradually come to grasp the enormity of what has been unconsciously revealed. And just when laughter and lightness are at their peak - laughter being particularly important to Herzberg - fear sets in.

Herzberg began her career as a writer for film and theatre in the '70's, when her reputation as a poet had already become established. For a few years she took part in a subsidised writing project which enabled her to write and workshop her plays under guidance. The value of this period for her is perhaps best measured by the quantity and quality of her work. Her script about the Jewish artist Charlotte Salomon, who died in Auschwitz, was made into a film. Her first full-length play *Leedvermaak*, looking at the attempts of several generations of a Jewish family to come to terms with the trauma of the war, became a huge success in Holland and Germany. She recently wrote a sequel.

The monologue included here, *The Caracal (De Caracal)*, should perhaps be seen in the context of a number of plays dealing with the problems of relationships in their widest sense: love, marriage, infidelity, parents and children, sisters, brothers. A woman spends the evening on the telephone and talks to her lovers, her sisters, an obscene caller, her late mother (through a medium) and the wife of her one great love whom she is expecting. He has promised to call her that evening, after a period of separation, to tell her his decision about the relationship - we wait with her. Meanwhile a picture of her life begins to emerge: her innate authority as headmistress of a school for children with behavioural problems, her efforts to free herself from the tentacles of her sisters, (one of whom has immersed herself in the world of the supernatural and the other who has, through sheer boredom, become involved with an academic with a less than savoury body odour). A Woody Allen-style fight evolves between the sisters about who has the greater right to use the bedroom. On top of all this, we learn that one of her pupils has run away and we wonder where he can be. The waiting continues. Her lover's wife tells her he left home months ago. Eventually the phone rings ... The end of the play wrong-foots us: rather we realise we have been wrong-footed all along. But what is right? Fascinated and intrigued, we share Herzberg's confusion about the unpredictability of human behaviour.

The other three plays deal with clearly recognisable social problems: incest, female eating disorders and the death of an AIDS patient. Typically of Dutch drama, this doesn't take place within a traditional realistic convention. As opposed to a progressive build-up of narrative drive, culminating in conflict, the writers offer a structure in which past and present are mixed. In one sense, everything has already happened. The present of the drama looks at what has already passed and how these events are remembered by the various characters. This narrative, epic style has as its consequence that no psychological certainty exists. What emerges is the way in which the personal history of the characters leads them to their various forms of survival: possibilities, choices and solutions.

Write me in the Sand (Schrijf me in het zand) by Inez van Dullemen (b. 1925) deals with Judith's discovery of what lay behind her older sister Anne's suicide, years before. As she is cleaning out her old bedroom, she comes across Anne's papers which reveal her loneliness, confusion, resentment and self-loathing. Suffering abuse at her father's hands for years, the girl is no longer sure who she is: 'Am I Anne or am I mummy, both daughter and woman, daughter and mother.' In a series of flashbacks in which the father and the young Anne appear, Judith gradually adds to her memories: what she remembers seeing but not understanding, and what she has hidden away. Her mother seeks to excuse herself by revealing secrets about her marriage - she married young to an older divorcée, who lost interest in her after the children were born. When Judith confronts her about her husband's abuse, she admits she was aware of it but hid herself away behind the mask of respectability. Anne's flight from the family home never offered a solution - she felt herself complicit because of her own sexual feelings. The final scene ends in stalemate: the unholy bond between the parents cannot be broken and Judith leaves for good. In a particularly subtle way (hence the success of the play), van Dullemen knows how to make this disturbed family tangible. Although 'absent', it is Anne who directs our view, who shows us how destructive the mental and physical violation of a young girl by the adult man is; through Judith, society's bewilderment is given a voice so that the collective mourning process can begin.

In the same way the structure of *Dossier: Ronald Akkerman* is a kind of mediation between direct and reported action. Writer Suzanne van Lohuizen (b.1953), already known internationally as a playwright for children, was commissioned to write the play by the René Klein Stichting, an organisation dealing with the terminal care of AIDS patients. The play opens with a young nurse arriving home from the funeral of a former patient who opted for assisted suicide - euthanasia being a choice she found hard to condone. She begins to speak about herself in the third person (She) and gradually a second voice (He) is woven in. As they drink coffee and he inspects her flat, she realises she has never seen him as a person because his decline had already become advanced when they met. Through a mixture of narration and dialogue, they reconstruct the period they spent together. They recreate her fear of AIDS patients and his fear of death, the way her business-like manner and petty rules drove him mad, and how he tried to go on living life to the full, all the while seriously ill and yet making miraculous recoveries. He experienced difficulties with his family who simply couldn't let him go, she looked after him during his final decline. He came to dominate her life and she feared that he would be dead after her return from holiday. The worst thing, she says, 'was that I came to love you. So full of joy, so still full of plans. And you, lovely to everyone, except to me ...' This apparent dialogue, which is actually a monologue, brings the She-character to an understanding of what actually happened to her during this period. Her ambivalent reaction following the funeral: 'singing with relief' and 'whining like a dog' thus finds its place at the beginning and end of her story.

Matin van Veldhuizen's approach to female eating-disorders in the appropriately named *Eat (Eten)*, is first and foremost light and humorous. Van Veldhuizen is as much an actress as a director and writer; she began her theatre career with a much talked about production of Jane Bowles in which three actresses played not only Jane, but also her mother, her famous husband Paul and her female lover, all three being intractable parts of Jane, as portrayed in her autobiography. In her search for the causes of madness and self-destruction in women, van Veldhuizen wrote, among others, about the German early romantic poetess de Kunderode, Dorothy Parker and the black sisters from 'Silent Twins.' In *Eat* we are introduced to three sisters and their various problems with food and body: one is bulimic, one anorexic and the third a constant weight-watcher. On the anniversary of their mother's death, they meet and unravel the causes of their eating disorders, locating the root of the problem in the relationship between their late mother and step-father. Despite the many current insights into eating disorders van Veldhuizen weaves into her play, it never becomes didactic - the women are very much alive and kicking. Aggression, rivalry and empathy each take their turn as difficulties arise; memories of the past are effortlessly followed by modern slogans and prescriptions about how to live. In this play, obsession with body and sexuality, go hand in hand, the one informing the attitude to the other. Moreover, it is not the narrative drive itself which engages but the stories which the three women construct for themselves as a legitimisation of what they have become. Their shaky self-knowledge is propped up by a large dose of irony, insight and everyday wisdom. The personal perception is most of all determined by culture.

It is this path - from the search for absolute truth to an attempt to survive in a story of one's own telling - which the writers and their characters have trodden. The time for fictional heroines is past. Being allowed and able to live must continually be fought for - every square inch of it.

Mieke Kolk

Dr Mieke Kolk is now senior lecturer for Theatre Studies at the University of Amsterdam. She worked for years as a theatre critic and was co-founder of the feminist theatre group Theatre Persona (1983-89). She has published several books on women and theatre, most recently *Speaking for Life: Female Subjectivity in Postmodern Theatre.* (1995)

WRITE ME IN THE SAND

by Incz van Dullemen
Translated by Anthony Akerman

Dutch premiere: Theater van het Oosten, 1989.
Director: Agaath Witteman
The play has been performed extensively in Europe and had its
German premiere in Munich in 1991.

CHARACTERS

Louis, the father
Linda, the mother
Judith, the youngest daughter, aged 22
Anne, the oldest daughter, aged 24
Psychiatrist
Anne's School Boyfriend
Child 1, the Young Anne
Child 2, the Young Judith

> I feel so bad, so lonely,
> so lost, so wrong.
> I need to hide underground,
> no room for my head.
> don't deserve to breathe,
> don't deserve room to exist in -
> In shallow land
> please write,
> in the wind
> in the sand
> in the nothing under the sea.

Heather Hughes   *Kansas City 1982*

SCENE 1

*The set comprises an hallucinatory empty space in which certain
elements of a house have been deployed; a window frame, a large
mirror, a chest of drawers containing Anne's past. Perhaps there are
two levels: a slightly raised platform upstage on which two
children's chairs are placed. There are chairs and a table for the
domestic scenes.*

*The Father, partially paralysed by a stroke, sits in a wheelchair..
The Mother is much younger than the Father. Anne, the older
daughter, is already dead at the beginning of the play, but assumes
corporeal shape through the memories of the living and the diary
she left behind. The Father is in his chair playing chess with a
computer. He is heard mumbling to an invisible opponent.*

COMPUTER   Your turn your turn your turn.
FATHER   I'm going to attack your king's flank. Attack is the
   best form of defence.

   *(He lights a cigarette. The metallic voice of the computer is
   audible.)*

COMPUTER   Your turn your turn your turn.
FATHER   Why A-8? What have you got in mind? Do you want
   to make a sacrifice? You don't think you can put one over on me?
   That pawn is covered by two pieces.

   (Judith enters with a weekend bag and a large bunch of flowers.)
   *(She kisses her mother. She goes to her father and offers the
   flowers to him.)*

JUDITH   The last of the summer roses. From the garden.
FATHER   That's nice of you, darling.
   (He runs his hand fleetingly over her stomach.)
   How's my namesake? I'll hang a fat cigar in the canopy of the

cradle, then it's sure to be a boy.
(He laughs.)
That's what my father did every time my mother was pregnant and
she bore him five sons.

JUDITH Well, you obviously didn't do that before we were
born.

FATHER A small Louis ... that's all I've got to look forward to.
Otherwise I'm finished, Judith. My legs are as heavy as two sacks
of meal.

(They leave the Father.)
(The Mother arranges the flowers in a vase.)

SCENE 2

MOTHER I'm glad you've come to help me. I couldn't face it on
my own.

JUDITH You're looking well.

MOTHER I try to put on a brave face, for your father's sake. I
go swimming three times a week, so I sleep better.

JUDITH It doesn't do your figure any harm either.

MOTHER You should go too, now that you're expecting.
*(Without thinking the Mother toys with the pendant around her
neck. She sees Judith looking at it.)*
This was given to Anne when she was twelve and went to
secondary school.

(Silence.)

JUDITH How is Father coping?

MOTHER You can see for yourself. He plays chess.

JUDITH At least it takes his mind off things.

*(Judith and the Mother start moving around the room
indecisively.)*

MOTHER   If you want anything, you must just say so. We can't take it all with us.

JUDITH   I haven't got space for large pieces of furniture.

(Judith starts taking clothes out of the cupboard; boxes, tied-off bags.)

MOTHER   They're as good as new. She hardly ever wore them. She always went for black clothes and chunky pullovers that did nothing for her.
(Takes a pullover and holds it up to Judith.)
It suits you. The turquoise goes with the colour of your eyes. She got it from your father for Christmas, but she said she couldn't stand the v-neck. Take it. You were about the same size.
(Judith takes the pullover and examines it briefly. Then she lets it fall to the floor).
Put what you don't want into those plastic bags. For the Salvation Army.
(Judith brings out a box and starts looking at photos. The Mother also looks at them.)

JUDITH   Photos of a children's party.

MOTHER   Yes, that's her wearing the top hat. Remember when she wanted to be a magician? Father bought her a conjurer's box as a present.

JUDITH   Would Daddy want this photo? Should I have it framed for him?

MOTHER   You'd better ask him that yourself.

JUDITH   Here she is next to the hollow tree she liked hiding in.

MOTHER   Oh God, the beer mug she's holding in her hand is still there in the kitchen.

JUDITH   Her school class. *(She reads the back of the photo.)* The Montessori Secondary School. That's the boyfriend she had then ... can't you see? Second from the left in the back row.

MOTHER   How on earth do you recognise the boy? My eyesight's so bad. Where are my glasses?

JUDITH   Why don't you wear them if your eyesight's so bad?

(The Mother looks around helplessly. Judith hands her the glasses.)

MOTHER I could never stand these glasses. As a child I never wanted to wear glasses because I felt so embarrassed.

JUDITH *(stares through the hole in the photo.)* She's cut herself out. There's a hole in ... Why do you think she did that?

MOTHER Perhaps she gave it to the boy.

(Silence.)

JUDITH Hey, the scissors. Didn't she use these to cut off her hair when she turned twelve? Father gave her a beating for that. She said she wanted to be a boy.

MOTHER Yes, she caused such a scene in the sports shop because she insisted on having baseball shoes and a boy's shirt.

(Judith finds a rag doll, a large crude clown.)

JUDITH Pako. Oh, he's lost an eye.

MOTHER He's falling to bits. He can be thrown away.
(She's about to put him in a plastic bag.)
It'll just collect moths.

JUDITH *(retrieves the doll.)* Poor Pako. He's been through such a lot with us.

MOTHER All the sawdust's falling out.

(Judith fiddles with the clown. White pills fall out of it. She feels inside the body, retrieves the pills from the floor.)

JUDITH Sleeping pills, codeine. Painkillers.
MOTHER How did they get in there?
JUDITH Were these yours? Were you taking these?
MOTHER What gives you that idea?
JUDITH Did she take them?

(The Mother doesn't reply.)
Oh, I can remember a night with a lot of running about and
commotion. Daddy made Anne throw up and you made strong
coffee.

MOTHER   Anne had a nervous tummy. She was always sick on
her birthday. Can't you remember her sitting there in the rocking-
chair under the party streamers, as white as a sheet, and sure
enough, she started her nonsense again and she had to be taken off
to bed and I stayed behind and played with you and the other
children.

(Judith looks from her Mother to the pills.)

JUDITH   How long would these have been in here?
MOTHER   She was always getting up to crazy things.

*(The Mother leaves the scene. The Father is isolated with his
game of chess. They are all isolated. Suddenly, for the first time,
Judith is confronted by the past. She walks around.)*

JUDITH   The house of our childhood. It's still here, full of
things from the past, full of memories. Unreal, like the silence
before being hit by a bomb. Soon everything will vanish,
everything will dissolve, and then the moving men will arrive and
the contractor and the architect and the carpenter, to change
everything - only the carcass will remain standing.
(Judith spreads her fingers and looks at them.)
Whoever is now alone will remain so for a long time. That's what
you always said, Anne ... A quotation from Rilke.
(She passes her hands along the wall.)
Our children's voices resounded between these walls. It's an
archaeological house. You either found the room too small or too
big. You were never satisfied by its proportions. You threw the
windows open. You said it stank. You mopped the floor with beer
to make it shine, or stuck silver paper onto the walls.

(She retrieves the pullover off the floor and looks in the mirror holding it in front of herself.)

I'm expecting a child ... We were two railroad coaches travelling along the same rails, but you derailed and plunged into the abyss. I'm still on the rails.

(Judith folds the pullover. She finds an eyebrow pencil.)

Payot - your brand. Payot Number Three.

(She looks in the mirror and accentuates her eyebrows with the pencil.)

Remember? When Mummy wasn't looking we stole her make-up things and painted each other's faces.

SCENE 3

Change of lighting. Anne enters. She is dressed in black and has a dark weal around her neck. Judith sees her image reflected in the mirror. A moment of arrested silence and concentration, while the sisters regard each other in the mirror. From this point onwards Anne will constantly be present, somewhere: far upstage, with her back to the audience, etc. Anne crosses to the rocking-chair and sits, rubs her hand on the armrest.

ANNE   My magician's chair, a good chair ... From here I can rule, judge, pass sentence. I can't leave this magician's chair. Whoever sits in it is protected from all evil.

JUDITH   You don't look any older than twelve. You're wearing the baseball shoes.   *(She points at her feet.)*

ANNE   They were bought to grow into.

(She picks up a counterpane from the floor and wraps herself in it.)

I'm always cold. I always put on two pairs of pyjamas ... Every night I wrap my old counterpane around me, like a cocoon, very tightly, so he can't find me. I sleep like a hare with my ears pricked ... His footsteps resonate through all the walls, even when he walks barefoot.

JUDITH   Who walks barefoot?

ANNE *(laughs.)* Here are silent snakes, tiny ones that adapt
themselves to the colour of the stones. There are also night snakes
that roam about in the night and adapt themselves to the dark.
They are the most dangerous. You must inoculate yourself against
their poison.

JUDITH   Who walks barefoot?

ANNE   Taking my scissors, I cut a red notch in my wrist.
Not really deep, but it bled profusely. I went to the bathroom to
wash it off: A small coral wound on my wrist. I shivered and said:
Ah, blood ... and watched the blood swirling away in the water.
After that I just went downstairs and ate a slice of bread with
peanut butter. Hate and love, peanut butter and blood ...

JUDITH   You also made a small wound in my wrist with the
same pair of scissors ...

ANNE   I said: Now you're also inoculated against the night
snake's poison.

JUDITH   You held my wrist to your mouth and sucked out the
blood. You said: We must always remember this day. We must
never let it out of our hearts. Now we're both inoculated against
sorrow.

(Silence. Anne crosses to the empty window frame.)

ANNE   Lying in bed at night I often looked up at the moon. I
imagined the moon looking down on me, I imagined I was the only
one who knew her ... we shared a secret. The moon was quite
detached from me, from my life, from what took place in this
house. She was there *outside.* I had long conversations with her.
But only when she was full.

JUDITH *(feels her stomach.)* Like me. *(They laugh.)*
*(Anne puts on a black top hat and executes a few dance
steps in front of the mirror.)*
You're not right in the head.

ANNE   My head ... ha ha. No, there's no logic in it. I wanted
to make you laugh. I always wanted to be a magician. You can
make miracles happen with thoughts. When fakirs concentrate they

leave the ground and levitate in the air. That's what I longed to do.
Most of all I wished I could make myself disappear.
So much has happened, but the things which have happened are
without beginning or end. They branch out in every direction.
*(Anne crosses to the two children's chairs, which stand in the
empty space facing each other.)*
Look, here are our children's chairs. Here we sat with our heads
facing each other so our foreheads and our noses touched. I
bathed myself in your warmth.

SCENE 4

*Music. Perhaps from an old music box? Or by Philip Glass? Two
small girls enter the circle of light and sit in the chairs with their
heads touching; they are dressed in white, slightly old-fashioned.
Anne and Judith remain outside the circle and speak the lines.*

JUDITH   You're squinting.
ANNE   You too. Ugh, my eyes are starting to hurt.
JUDITH   You're the mother. And I'm the child.

*(The smaller of the two girls applies lipstick to the elder, on and
around her mouth until it's a very large blood-red mouth. After
that she draws two circles on the elder's dress.)*

We're going on a picnic. You're going to light the fire.
ANNE   Pako can't come along. He's been naughty. Did you
know that? He murdered the father.
JUDITH   He must be punished.
ANNE   He must be punished. Should we throw him in the
fire?
JUDITH   No, not in the fire.
ANNE   Oh yes. He must die. Let's draw and quarter him.
(The young girls pull the doll. A leg comes off.)
JUDITH   It's your fault.
ANNE   It's my fault.

(She steps out of the role of young girl.)
It was always my fault. I was guilty, guilty every day. I had to pay
the price. I was always expected to know what was good or bad
and you weren't. You were always Mother's little angel.

JUDITH   But Father spoilt you. He gave you everything, white
boots for skating, a new bicycle. I always had to make do with
your cast-offs. He took you with him when he went on trips. To
Antwerp ... He always found an excuse for you to miss school.
You were so delicate. You had such a bad appetite. You always
had ways of twisting him around your little finger. Trickery, that's
what Mother always says: Anne is full of tricks ... Oh, at times I
hated you.

*(The young girls chase each other and hit each other with the
mutilated rag doll. The Father enters in his dressing-gown and
takes part in the romp. He goes and sits downstage and takes the
children on his lap.*

LITTLE GIRLS   Daddy, Daddy ...
FATHER   Would you like to hear a story? All right. Once upon
a time there was a little girl who was very disobedient and what's
more she was very curious. She didn't even believe children were
found under the gooseberry bush. One day the little girl said: 'They
say that a witch lives deep in the woods and that she can do all
sorts of wonderful things.' - 'Child, never go into the woods,' said
her father, 'they're full of menacing, terrible things.' - 'I'd like to
find out what they are,' said the disobedient little girl. And sure
enough, one day, when her father was taking a nap, she crept out
of the house and went into the woods. She'd never been there
before and very soon she was lost. There were hundreds of trees,
so she didn't know which direction she should take. She
walked and walked and suddenly she heard the bang of a gun and
dogs barking - that must be the woodsman. Perhaps he could tell
her where the witch lived. She crawled through the bushes and yes,
there was the woodsman standing between the trees. But no sooner
had he spotted her than he took aim, because you don't find such a

juicy little girl to shoot every day in the woods. He missed her, the bullet went right passed her, but the dog came trotting towards her with its red, wet tongue drooling out of its mouth. The little girl ran away, the brambles tore her skin open and she heard the woodsman calling, 'Catch her!' The woodsman's dog sank his big yellow teeth into her; she managed to pull herself away, but he had already taken a piece of flesh out of her thigh.

(Father imitates the dog with its tongue hanging out of its mouth. The young girls giggle.)

Fortunately, the disobedient girl could wade through a stream so the dog lost her scent. The disobedient girl walked further and further. Somewhere she saw the leaves moving - had the woodsman found her after all? No, it wasn't the woodsman. She walked towards a strange man, 'Oh kind sir, please will you help me? My dress is torn and covered in blood.' The strange man produced a knife. 'You're just in time, my piglet has run away and I'm looking for a juicy piece of meat. And the flesh of little girls is delicious too.' - 'Oh sir, please don't harm me, begged the little girl.' But he was already sharpening his knife. - 'That left breast of yours appeals to me, little girl's breast flavoured with parsley and thinly-sliced onion, mmmmmmm .... lightly fried so it's nice and brown and crispy.'

(The young girls tremble. The elder slides off his lap, but he takes her by the wrist as if he's the bad butcher.)

'Ah, just one little breast, surely you won't miss that?'

(He makes a gesture of severing a breast with a knife.)

The bad butcher put the breast in his knapsack and disappeared into the dark woods. The little girl struggled on. Far away in the distance she saw a light burning. An old woman stood in the doorway leaning on a stick. 'Oh,' called the disobedient little girl, 'please let me rest here for a moment. I'm so tired and I'm in such pain.' 'Oh, I can see that, said the old woman. She had a big, hooked nose, because who do you think she was?

LITTLE GIRLS   The witch, the witch ...

FATHER   Yes, that's who she was, the witch. She said, 'I already know who you are. You're the disobedient little girl. And because you didn't listen to your father, I'm now going to have to punish you.'

(The Father cuddles and tickles the young Anne. The adult Judith stands watching from a distance and sees how the young Anne lies limply against the Father, like a lifeless doll. The image freezes. Judith calls out as if she wakes from a dream.)

JUDITH   Why are you dead?

(She runs from the domain of the two children's chairs - the domain of the past - to the cupboard and holds Pako to her stomach. The young girls have disappeared.)

SCENE 5

JUDITH   Why are you dead? *Dead?*

(Mother enters, puts her arms around Judith. They lean against one another. Then they sit down. A serene, intimate scene.)

MOTHER   Daddy wants to give her a very special gravestone. It has to come all the way from Brittany. Because Anne loved Brittany so much ... From Mont St. Michel, where it rises from the sea. At low tide you can walk out there across the sand. The summer before last she lived there in a holiday house on the coast. The stone has to be hewn out of those rocks.

JUDITH   That's a lovely idea.
(Silence.)

MOTHER   We've done everything, everything that lay within our
power...
(Silence.)
Her psychiatrist said she had a leaking ego - that's what he called
it. A leak in her ego through which her life force ebbed away.
(Silence.)
Let's hope that - wherever she is - she's found peace. Perhaps it's
for the best ... Someone who really wants to, will do it anyway,
sooner or later. You can't stop them. Sometimes the patients are
even cheerful, according to the psychiatrist. You don't notice
anything's wrong and suddenly they do it all the same.

JUDITH   You haven't told me *where ...*

MOTHER *(with averted face)* In the garage.

JUDITH   Were you at home?

MOTHER   I had my bridge evening.

JUDITH   And father?

MOTHER   Was in front of the t.v. She was back home for the
first time. She seemed better than in a long while.
(Silence.)
She was always a strange child. She did weird drawings of
embryos with a black dagger sticking into their little bodies.

JUDITH   But why?...

MOTHER   Maybe now he'll be able to love her again ...

JUDITH   What's that supposed to mean?

MOTHER   Maybe now he'll be able to remember her the way she
was when she was a child.

(The Mother exits. Judith starts stacking boxes.)
*(Lighting change. A light comes on above the Father. Judith
crosses to the Father. She looks at the chess board.)*

JUDITH   Are you playing with white? Do you think you can
beat him?

FATHER   It's bloody hard. Now I'm playing the advanced class.
(Silence.)
You've heard my blood pressure's getting better? I'm getting worse

but my blood pressure's getting better ...
(He laughs.)

JUDITH   Mother told me you want to give her a special gravestone, from Brittany ...

FATHER   Yes. And perched on top of that I'd like a small, white
dove. Like the one perched on top of my kid sister's tombstone.
We had a lot of dead people in our family ... When I was a kid I
had to go to the florist every Sunday and take the flowers my
father had ordered to the cemetery. I liked it there. It was peaceful.
I sat on the iron chains which were hung around the graves. I used
to sit there swinging on them. The verger caught me. He put a stop
to that.
(Silence. The Father stares at the chess board.)

JUDITH   How was she? Did she say anything that last
evening?

FATHER *(staring at the chess board.)* What evening are you
talking about?

JUDITH   Before she ... in the garage ...
(The Father keeps staring at the chess board.)

FATHER   B-3, then I'll keep his knight pinned down. Yes, that's
a good move.

JUDITH   Father ... I asked you something.

FATHER   Spare me this, please.

JUDITH   I'm sorry. *(She returns to the cupboard area and
picks up the broken Pako.)*
(Silence)
Why do I know so little about you? How did we become so
estranged, after growing up under the same roof ...? You just
stepped off ... But we have to go on living with this horror ...

*(She is about to push Pako into a plastic bag, almost angry,
irritated, but suddenly has second thoughts. She takes the pair of
scissors, cuts the body open and takes out a wad of papers. She
unfolds them. She reads:)*
'This is my self portrait, the portrait of my life. Perhaps it will end
up in a trash can with Pako and that's the way it should be.

Whatever happens to Pako happens to me too. My life belongs in
a trash can. This bizarre life of mine, this life of stone. Judith
thinks I'm sick too, sick in the head. That's what they told her. She
asks if I sleep well and I always say I do. I don't want her to go
through what happened to me. I always carry my scissors in my
socks, or in the pocket of my jeans and if I have to, I'll kill him.
Or perhaps it would be better to sneak into the garage at night and
set fire to the pornographic magazines he hides there, so the car
explodes and the whole house goes up in flames and I'd quickly get
Judith out of bed and run down the stairs with her while the flames
begin to crackle. And we two would carry on living, quite alone.'
*(Judith looks around her. There is no-one there. She continues
reading:)*
'All I know is my own history. I look through a glass wall at the
child who has locked me up. I see her gesticulating, screaming,
crying, telling absurd jokes and playing the fool.'

*(Anne is now standing in front of the mirror looking at her
image.)*

I am her and I am not her.
For her, the child, time has stood still. She has no future and no
past. I stand in front of the mirror and slash the flesh of my arm
with my scissors. Red pearls of blood swell up on my skin. The
pain glows deliciously - the child behind the glass writhes and
laughs - and briefly we are one, she and I.'

*(Judith quickly hides the papers as the Mother enters to collect
something.)*

SCENE 6

Lighting change. The Father is in a spotlight.

COMPUTER Your turn your turn your turn. Your turn your turn
your turn.

FATHER   You're not going to catch me out like that. I'm a sly old fox. I'm going to outflank you ...

COMPUTER   Your turn your turn your turn.

FATHER   Take it easy. (*He moves a knight.*)

Peeeeace. Over all the mountain tops is peace... Isn't that how it went? *Peeeeace* ... like the sighing of the wind in the tree tops.

(*The light in the Father's area becomes increasingly intense and the rest of the stage becomes darker. We hear a murmur. It becomes louder. It sounds like falling water. Water falling from a shower. It would be effective if the smell of jasmine floated into the auditorium. A projection of a very young girl under a shower becomes discernible. The Father looks up from the chess board.*)

Wait now ... Oh, you are sweet ... I'll touch the skin of your body with my fingers, sprinkle it with water and dry it carefully, inch by inch, the way I used to polish my motorbike, inch by inch. My girl ... I see your hand wiping a clearing in the steam on the mirror, the moisture that runs in tears down your cheeks. I see you as if you were in a pond, under the surface of the water, your hands and your child-like body blurred, you let one little hand fall - that's the most beautiful thing of all, your empty hand dangling limply at your side.

(*The sound of the water becomes stronger.*)

When you were very small you rubbed that lovely body of yours up against me. You were made for love. Don't think you can hide away from me in that steam. Why won't you let me? You know it's going to happen, sooner or later. So stop teasing me. You don't want to spoil our fun, do you? Make me unhappy?

(*The sound of the shower stops. The projected image fades out.*)

I feel like a caged rat. Trapped. Trapped. Man wasn't born to be trapped between four walls.

(He knocks the computer to the floor, scattering the pieces. The computer continues mumbling 'Your turn your turn your turn.' He rings the emergency bell. The Mother appears.)
(Lighting change.)

MOTHER   Is anything wrong?

FATHER   I'll have to hire a nurse to put compresses on my head and massage my feet. I'm in agony and you make me wait.

MOTHER   I can't be in two places at once.

FATHER   I'm not interested in sweaters, slippers and shirts. I'm racked with neuralgia, convulsions, cramps in my legs and my head.

MOTHER   Shall I wet a towel for you? That'll be cool and refreshing.

FATHER   Jesus God, not now. I need air.

MOTHER   I'll open the window.

FATHER   If only I'd kicked it ... Then I wouldn't be such a bloody nuisance.

(The Mother goes down on her knees to gather up the chess pieces.)

Just give me my pills.

(The Father takes the pills.)

What use is this crap? They're all quacks, those doctors.

(He tries to lift one of his legs.)

I think this leg is heavier than my other. You think that's possible? I can't even move my left foot because I can't reach it. I sit here chained to my chair and wait. Today it's my leg. Tomorrow it'll be my head that'll bloat up like a *Mardi Gras* puppet.

MOTHER   Shall I massage your neck for you? You always liked that.

FATHER   No, I need rest. I must sleep, sleep. Leave me alone. Is that asking too much?

(The Mother gives the Father her arm and leads him away.)

SCENE 7

Music. Lighting change. The domain of the night. Anne sits in the rocking-chair, wrapped in her counterpane. Lights up on Judith. She takes a letter out of an envelope and begins to read.

JUDITH   I act out a role every day of my life. I conceal a mass of dark things under my magician's cloak. If you've acted out a role, your entire life - because I was a cunning little liar from the age of six or seven ... then you're branded. A year ago now, Judith, when you listened to me in the garden while you pruned the roses, I felt like clutching your hand and letting the tears come finally after all those years. But I couldn't give sound to the words. They stuck in my throat. It seemed as if we were sitting on a see-saw. You went up. I saw you in the light air. And I sank down, because I'm worthless, dirty, contaminated. I must go under the earth. I can't speak to you about what's going on inside me. The distance between us is too great.

(Judith turns the pages, reads.)

September eighteen. I've been writing all night long and *he* is sleeping next to Mummy ... Honour thy father and thy mother, that's one of the ten commandments. I can't even think about Mummy. She always out-argues me, but she never listens to what I have to say. My words seem to be a cold wind that chills her. Sometimes I see her staring out of the window without seeing anything and then I know that nothing will ever change for either of us. She'll be sitting somewhere waiting for old age and I'll be sitting in the madhouse waiting for insanity.

(Judith lowers the pages and stares ahead of her. The young Anne with her blood-red mouth enters and sits on one of the chairs. Judith reads.)

Am I Anne or am I Mummy, both daughter and woman, daughter and mother? She lives in me and I in her, my mother, female parent, my beginning or my end? Who am I?

(The Father enters in his pyjamas and stands behind the little girl.)

FATHER *(Whispers)* Daddy's baby, Daddy's princess. Unbutton your dress....

ANNE His fingers, dark nicotine stained, trace the round swelling.
(The Father draws the child between his knees and traces the round circles on the dress.)
They move as softly as a whisper over the small curves, slowly they go up and down, up and down. He cups one with his hand.

FATHER You're going to have nice little tits. You're becoming a woman, sweetheart....

ANNE His breathing becomes fast, as if he had a fever. His eyes bore into my body. My nipples are like swelling sores. When I look down at them I don't understand it.

YOUNG ANNE Daddy ... are we bad?

FATHER What makes you think that? I've told you everyone does it.

YOUNG ANNE Then why can't I tell anyone?

FATHER Because it's our little secret. You can keep a secret, can't you? And don't tell Mummy or you'll make her sad.

(Dance music. The Father waltzes with the little girl.)

I know women like to put up a struggle. But you mustn't struggle too much, because then something could go wrong.

(The Father and young Anne are frozen in their dance position, as if locked in time.)

JUDITH *(Reading)* 'Everything sways slowly in my head. I try to detach my feelings from the lifeless doll clamped between his thighs. I close my eyes tightly and try to recite all the capital cities of Europe. After a while the quickness always begins, the quickness of movement, blood rushing in my ears, and then the moment comes that hurts the most, because it's now so very quick … And then it's as sharp as a knife, and then it ends. All at once I return to the surface and everything that was blood-red and murky now seems caught in sharp lines: his big wet head, his mouth lolling open …'

FATHER   One two three, one two three, this is our classical dance, but you must let me lead … One two three….

(Then the lights fade and the Father and young Anne disappear.)

ANNE   You lied. Other fathers and daughters don't do this. I'm the *only one* in the whole world that *this happens to* … I didn't want to, but I did do it. Imagine if it gets out? What must I say? Who would ever believe me?
(She stands in front of the mirror and looks at herself.)
I don't want to have tits. He keeps looking to see if they're growing, every time he barges in while I'm taking a shower - the bolt in the bathroom is broken. I know he broke it on purpose. He's promised to repair it, but he keeps putting it off. I barricade the inside of the door with a chair, but Mother says: 'Stop making such a fuss. Surely you've got nothing to hide …'

JUDITH *(Reading the diary)* 'I thought I was abnormal. No-one in my class had breasts yet. I was all alone, as if I belonged to another species. I had to enter that other country alone, the world where fingers groped in places that had never been touched before and now suddenly had hypersensitive skin cells as if they had a life all of their own. I hated my body, because it became a thing that wasn't mine, but belonged to *him.*'
(Judith lights a cigarette and allows the smoke to escape from between her lips as if it were a white tongue.)
Pages from a jotter, letters that were never posted … All those

cuttings from your life, those fragments, Anne ... as if you were torn to shreds and I have to stick all the pieces of your life back together again. No, I don't want to read on.
(She sits with her hands around her head as if trying to look back in time.)
Everything becomes obscene ... an enormous, filthy stain spreading over everything ... You'd have been better off if you'd fallen under a train.

SCENE 8

Mother enters wearing a nightgown. Judith hides the papers.

MOTHER   Can't you sleep either? Is it because of the baby?
(Judith shakes her head.)
Can I make you something? Hot milk? Or would you like an orange? Are you getting enough vitamins?
JUDITH   Stop worrying.
MOTHER   Your eyes are red.
JUDITH   I've been reading.
MOTHER   What?
JUDITH   Our old book of fairy tales.

(Silence)

MOTHER   Are you and your boyfriend happy together?
JUDITH   We get along just fine.
MOTHER   I don't really know him. Why haven't you brought him here more often?
JUDITH   We live in a different world. I don't want to expose him to father's critical eye. He just sits there in judgement, deciding whether his daughters' boyfriends belong to the same superior race he thinks he belongs to, socially successful and all that ... I can still remember how he showed the door to the only boyfriend Anne ever had.
MOTHER   He thought she was still too young.

JUDITH   Too young? At sixteen? He used to hide behind the curtains and if he saw the boy riding his bicycle in front of the house, he ran downstairs to ask him who he was looking for. And he told Anne that if he ever saw the boy near the house again, he would tell him a few home truths, that she was a slut and tarted around on street corners ...

MOTHER   Judith, you're all we have left. You're expecting our first grandchild ... Don't you think we've finally earned the right to a little happiness?

JUDITH   Let's leave it now, Mummy. It's the middle of the night. It's all so new for me. And we must get some sleep.

MOTHER   There's something I can't get out of my mind. I keep seeing this image: how she slid out of me when she was born, a tiny blue child with an umbilical cord around her neck - a strong, grey tube with blood vessels. Her little face was dark and swollen.... It kept coming back to me when I saw that blue weal around her neck ... the umbilical cord, as if the time in between had fallen away.

That she chose to do it that way, without knowing about the umbilical cord... But the blouse with the high collar disguised it well. She looked lovely ... everyone said so. She looked at peace.

(Mother exits.)

SCENE 9

Judith is obsessively preoccupied with the papers. She places them around her on the floor. Anne walks into the circle of light.

ANNE   It's because of the dog collar I saw hanging from a gate by a little shed. The buckle was still fastened, but there was no dog in it. That reminded me of a noose. I'd also been thinking of drowning myself. Drowning doesn't take longer than five minutes, no longer than it takes to boil an egg, but hanging is faster, at least if you do it properly.

I dreamt I was sentenced to death. I told Father he could have my

body and told him where and when he could find it. Because that's
the procedure after an execution: family members are allowed to
collect the body.
A jury had sentenced me to death and I had to carry out the
sentence myself. The members of the jury sat in a long row in the
school desks from my junior school.

(Anne crosses the stage and looks into the audience.)

I recognised each and every one of them: the girls in my class who
had now become women, and the teacher, the neighbours and my
therapist - For a moment I had a glimmering of hope because I
thought, 'They know I'm not guilty, that *he's* the one.' And yet
they all turned their thumbs down. I realised I'd been found guilty.
I walked up the stairs and in the attic the same empty dog collar
hung from a beam.
(She sits at the table with Judith and turns her wrist upwards.)
We're sisters. We carry the same scars.

JUDITH   I felt the scar draw tight the day you hanged yourself
in the garage.

ANNE   It was winter. I was cleansed and pure, not bad.
(Silence)
He bought me a diaphragm when I was twelve.

JUDITH   I don't believe you.

ANNE *(Laughs briefly)* He said, 'You must use this from now on,
because if you don't you might have a baby and it'll be a monster
with two heads or deaf and dumb. And then I'll have to go to
prison and you'll be sent to a reformatory for bad girls ...' Until
then it had seemed like a weird game, a dirty game of course ... but
from the moment he entered me for the first time, he destroyed
everything. He only saw my body and not the little girl I really
was. He just didn't care. I thought, 'if I'd become paralysed from
my waist down, I'd feel nothing and only live on in my mind ...
then my body would be dead.'
*(She stands and takes a few steps in the direction of the rocking-
chair.)*

But you can also fuck a dead body....

(Judith walks away with her hand in front of her mouth as if she wants to throw up. The sound of a lavatory being flushed.)

SCENE 10

Morning. The Father rolls himself towards the table in the wheelchair. The Mother places the roses in the middle of the table and sets the places for breakfast. Father starts reading the morning paper.

FATHER   The police finally caught the guy who strangled Betty Visser in the toilet after he'd raped her. It was the barman at the disco where Betty had been all night. You hear that, Linda? What's a kid of that age doing in a disco late at night? Today they just do as they please. We need an iron fist to get the kids back into line ... You can see it all around you. What these kids need is another war. Then they'll find out what it's all about: discipline ... They don't appreciate what they've got and they don't know how good they've got it either ...

MOTHER *(Calling)* Judith! Are you finished? Breakfast's ready.
    (She sits down at the table.)

FATHER *(Laughing)* Dog bites man's nose off ... That's it, good boy ... The victim was walking along the sidewalk when the dog, a small breed of Rottweiler, suddenly went for his face. The animal disappeared without trace.
    (To Mother.)
    He probably had a score to settle with that guy. Rottweilers are smart. They never forget an insult ...

(Judith enters and sits down at the table without looking up when she greets them.)

JUDITH   Good morning. Fresh raisin bread ...
    (To Mother)

Did you bake it yourself?

MOTHER   To celebrate that you're home again. Like old times.

FATHER   You have to eat for two. Little Louis must grow up
to be a tough guy.

JUDITH   Who says he's going to be called Louis?
(They eat. The Mother pours tea.)
Perhaps it'll be a girl.

MOTHER   Why are you eating so little? Are you still having
morning sickness?

JUDITH   Every now and then.
(The clatter of cutlery.)

FATHER   There was a hell of a wind last night. It kept me
awake.

MOTHER   I'll be glad when we've left this place. Father's
getting an adapted bathroom. He'll be able to go to the toilet by
himself ...

*(The clatter of cutlery. Young Anne enters holding a ball and
joins them at the table. Mother addresses her.)*

Finish your food.

YOUNG ANNE I don't want anymore.

MOTHER   I slave away to serve up something decent and you
turn your nose up at it.

YOUNG ANNE It tastes like cat shit.

*(With her feet she rolls the ball back and forth under the table.
Mother looks under the table.)*

MOTHER   What have you got there?

YOUNG ANNE A ball. Daddy gave it to me.

MOTHER   Give here.
(To Father.)
You shouldn't give her a ball to play with just before we sit down
to eat.

FATHER   Bunk.

MOTHER   Why do you speak to me like that, when you know how concerned I am ...?

(To Young Anne.)

Open your mouth. Swallow.

(Young Anne retains the food in her cheeks and doesn't swallow.)

You haven't done your homework ... I've heard the whole story, so don't try to get out of it ... If you carry on like this, you'll flunk. Swallow.

(Young Anne spits everything out.)

Little bitch.

(Gives her another mouthful.)

Swallow.

(To the Father.)

She does it on purpose, not eating ... trying to upset me. Speak to her, Louis. She's just an actress playing her little games.

FATHER   She's just more sensitive than you are. You've got no sense of smell. You can't smell that the porridge is burnt. Cat shit....

(He laughs. Judith kicks the ball under the table and it rolls across the stage ... Young Anne runs after it and disappears. The Father wheels himself away in his chair. Music sounds.)

SCENE 11

A while later. Lights fade up. The Mother and Judith sit at the table.

JUDITH   So you stole him away from another woman?

MOTHER   I was eighteen ... I wanted to keep the baby. But I was also scared. Scared of having to bring it up by myself.

JUDITH   Why didn't you have an abortion? Or were you trying to force him to marry you?

MOTHER   Abortion ... Today you talk about it as if it were nothing, but in my day it was a sin.

JUDITH   I can't imagine how you could ever have married him.

MOTHER   Why are you suddenly so down on him?

JUDITH   You've got more reason to hate him than I have.

MOTHER   I don't know what you're getting at ...

JUDITH   You've never shown your real feelings. You kept a whole pile of masks in your cupboard and you used to hide behind them.

(She makes a gesture as if tearing a mask off her Mother's face. Then she runs her hand roughly through her Mother's hair leaving it tousled.)

You can't hide anymore, behind prissiness and make-up.

MOTHER   Don't be so spiteful. You're tired. We're both dead-beat.

JUDITH   You knew about Father and her, but you kept your mouth shut. You didn't lift a finger to protect her.

MOTHER   What are you talking about? Your father was crazy about Anne. No-one knows that better than you. It made you jealous. Don't try and deny it.

JUDITH   Now I see what a liar you are. You know exactly what I'm talking about ... Did it never occur to you that he couldn't keep away from her, that he went through to her bedroom late at night...?

MOTHER   To kiss her goodnight - it was a habit since she was small.

JUDITH *(Derisive)* A goodnight kiss!

MOTHER   Perhaps your father didn't always keep his hands to himself, but that's all ... Ever since she was a child Anne always dramatised everything....

(Silence)

Good God, Judith... You know Anne was sick, mentally disturbed, that she was hysterical and a compulsive liar. I'm not saying that to blame her. She couldn't help herself, the poor child ...

JUDITH   It's as if I've hooked a thread and everything's unravelled. The entire invisible fabric. I keep hearing Anne's stifled sobs. You said; 'Nowadays she cries at the drop of a hat.

It's the age.' How old was I? Seven or eight? You were in hospital. 'Daddy will look after you,' you said. It was summer. A sultry summer night. I couldn't sleep. It's crazy that I suddenly remember it now after all these years. Anne's bed was empty. I walked to yours and Daddy's bedroom. I held the doorknob in my hand ... behind it was something that told me not to make a noise. Through a crack in the door I saw Anne standing on your double bed. She had on tennis socks and the hairs on her legs glistened because she was positioned like she was standing in front of a floodlight. Her arms hung limply at her sides and slowly Daddy began to undo the buttons on her dress. His clumsy fingers had trouble with the buttonholes. He undressed her as if she was a doll. They were playing at undressing dolls and I wasn't allowed to join in. The dress moved up, over Anne's head. So did her vest. She had swollen nipples on her chest ... Daddy kissed them, licked around them with his tongue. The crazy thing was that Anne didn't move. She looked like a statue being worshipped, a small white statue, disdainful, that pony tail of hers falling on her back. I felt a sharp pang of jealousy because the two of them were playing a secret game and I was shut out. Then Daddy pulled down her panties ...

MOTHER   I don't want to hear it. I didn't hear it.

JUDITH   Perhaps you know what happened next? He did something to his own clothes and suddenly his pants fell in a pool around his ankles ... I had to bite my knuckles to contain my laughter and my excitement. He put Anne down on the bed. I could see her feet ...

MOTHER   I'm not listening.

JUDITH   You will listen. You're going to hear what happened to your daughter. Daddy crawled on top of her and I was mesmerised by those feet in tennis socks, moving back and forth between. Daddy's legs like little animals.

   I couldn't understand what was happening. I cried myself to sleep because I felt so lonely. While Anne was allowed to sleep in the big bed with Daddy. The alarm clock went off in the morning, the sun shone and I heard Daddy whistling while he warmed up the

milk for our cornflakes. He came in carrying the teapot. He said,
'We can get along just fine without Mummy ... what do you say?'

MOTHER   Did he say that?

JUDITH   What did you know? Did you catch them in the act?
In bed? In the basement, in the car, in the garage? Or did you
close your eyes because you didn't want to catch them? You were
the woman of the house. That's the halo he gave you and you
wore it gratefully, because it kept you safe, safe and dead behind
that facade.

MOTHER   Do you think I haven't been through my own hell?
Sometimes I dreamt she was a baby again and that I drowned her
in the toilet, that I pulled the chain and flushed her down the sewer.
It's the same dream I had when I was eighteen and panicked
because I found out I was pregnant ... During the day I felt guilty
and confused, but in my dream I flushed her down the sewer.

JUDITH   Admit it ... You can't hide behind one of your masks.
You've shattered the entire myth of devoted motherhood yourself.
There's a gaping chasm between your so-called 'virtue' and your
motherhood. Maybe you didn't care that he was fooling around
with her, because it meant you didn't have to go to bed with him?

MOTHER   God knows what I've had to put up with. I was in
hospital after my third miscarriage ... that time I nearly bled to
death ... and all the time he was having his way ... with her.

(Silence)

JUDITH   He sent me to the florist to buy chrysanthemums for
you. White chrysanthemums. He gave me a ten-guilder note.

MOTHER   He knows I detest chrysanthemums - flowers for the
dead, that's what my mother called them. When I came home from
hospital I was so weak he had to lift me out of the taxi and help me
up the stairs. He gave Anne a look that somehow seemed to have
to do with me. Suddenly I saw myself through his eyes: sick,
ashen, finished. I saw those two standing together: my husband
and the child conceived during our first nights together. For the
first time it struck me how much she had started to look like me.

They seemed like allies and I was a visitor from another world.

JUDITH   How could it have happened?

MOTHER   I got the shock of my life one day, as I was folding up
her night dress - it had a smell, the smell of raw mushrooms ... I
told myself I was imagining things. But something froze inside
me. Whenever he touched me I smiled apologetically. And he was
only too happy to give me the blame: *I was frigid.*
Gradually I became locked into the role. Was he mocking me?
Did he really not see how humiliated I was? He always said I was
a woman who castrated him. He blamed me for not being able to
function properly.
But he...he has a very small thing down there, for a man with his
robust build. The other day at my niece's I saw her baby's little
dick under his fat tummy and I burst out laughing and tears came
to my eyes.

(She laughs, a nervous laugh.)

JUDITH   Did you ever love him?

MOTHER   I had no idea how I felt about anything. I didn't
know if I loved him or if he was the one I wanted. I only knew that
someone had turned up who said that *he* loved *me.* I was
inexperienced. I knew nothing about men. I felt flattered that he
took me into his confidence and told me intimate things about his
life, about his disillusionment with his marriage. I felt sorry for
him. He seemed friendly and in some ways vulnerable.

(She lights a cigarette.)

I felt attracted to him ... but he also repelled me and I didn't know
exactly why ... One day - not long after we were married - he
bought me a sapphire ring. I often left it in its box, but every day
he asked me how I liked the ring. If he didn't see it on my finger,
he'd ask, 'Where's my ring?' 'I just took it off to do the washing-
up,' I said, 'I'll put it on right away.' He told everyone he'd given
me the ring and in that way he made people feel that everything I
had came from him, the housekeeping money and the house and the
garden and even the air I breathed. There were times when I
wanted to throw that damned ring back in his face. But he was so
much older and more experienced. I didn't have my own identity,

my own opinions. I even got my ideas from him. I gradually came
to despise myself and my own sex. When we were just married he
always wanted to play games with me. I had to dress up like a
junior school kid in knee-length socks and a short skirt. I plaited
my hair and tied it off with ribbons. He wanted me to ring the
doorbell and then I had to say, 'Oh, sir, I've lost my way ... please
could you help me?' He let me in and I had to sit next to him on
the sofa with my skirt pulled up. He insisted that I kept calling
him 'sir', as if he was a stranger, and he called me, 'child,' and all
the while I talked as if I really was a little girl and I had to resist
when he tried to fondle me ... Then he plied me with beer and I had
to pretend to pass out, while he undressed me so he could have his
way with me. One night he turned on the tape recorder and I had
to make all sorts of sexual noises, which he recorded. My God,
why am I telling you all this?

JUDITH   Perhaps you also enjoyed it.

MOTHER   I only wanted one thing. to make your father happy
and make him love me. I felt so insecure because he'd already left
one woman. I thought he would love me if I gave myself to him
completely, gave him everything he asked for.
(*She fiddles with her pendant.*)
What did I do wrong? How did this happen to me?

JUDITH   Why didn't you divorce him?

MOTHER   Who can you blame for what's happened? Your
father? Anne? Me...? Whose fault was it? What difference does
it make whose fault it was, I'll still have to take the blame. And all
these years I've served your father loyally.

JUDITH   Served? That service has done more harm than if
you'd stood up to him. Didn't you have any pride at all?

MOTHER   What's pride? What does that entail? I couldn't bear
feeling so worthless, so unloved ... Tell me what I should
have done? Charge him? Drag him into court? Of course he
would have denied it. Should I have disgraced my family? Torn it
apart? I still had you ... I didn't want to burden you with the
image of a loathsome father. There were times when I was on the
point of leaving with the two of you ... But where would I have

gone? Anyway he would have been able to find me. I hushed it up
for your sake, so you'd have a care-free childhood. If you take
that away from me, I might just as well go out and cut my throat.

JUDITH   You're too much of a coward for that.

MOTHER   All those years I carried you on my shoulders through
the mire. I didn't want anyone to find out what was happening
here behind these doors. I was being dragged under. I desperately
looked for firm ground. But my suspicions grew, because there
was always that smell.

JUDITH   The smell of raw mushrooms? Sometimes Anne had
bruises on her neck, on her legs, and she'd say she'd been
sleep-walking again and had bumped into something.

MOTHER   She did walk in her sleep. And she hurt herself
deliberately. I was always worried about her.

(Suddenly aggressive.)

Why do you treat me as if I'd done God alone knows what? He
committed a crime, not me. At times I was even scared when I lay
next to him in bed. He'd become a stranger to me. Who knows
what he could have done? He abused me just as much as he
abused Anne. It was even harder for me than for her. He often
took her with him on business trips to Paris, to Antwerp, but I had
to stay at home and answer the phone when his business associates
called. I lived as if I was trapped in a block of ice.

(Silence.)

JUDITH   Are you quite sure you did it for me? Weren't you
scared of losing your status as a respectable matron? Didn't you
sacrifice everything for that? So you could go through life
unblemished, with your good reputation and good income intact?

MOTHER   You're pregnant ... maybe you're carrying your own
rival inside you ... a small soft monster that will depose you, steal
your husband and turn you into a sexless creature, a slave in your
own house. If you knew that for a fact, would you still want it to
be born?

JUDITH *(becomes pale)* I'd fight to make sure that it never happened.

MOTHER   It's elusive. It follows its own course, stealthily ... You don't believe it. You can't believe it. In my wildest dreams I could never conceive of something like that. It went beyond my power of imagination. At home we never talked about sex. It was taboo. We were never affectionate towards each other, never even kissed each other. There was no time for that kind of nonsense. We had a strict Catholic upbringing. I was still a virgin when your father started his love-making.

JUDITH   Anne wasn't born a small soft monster. You and father turned her into one. He's the monster. And you took sides with him against your own daughter. Deep down inside you're probably glad she's dead. Go on, admit it ... My god. It would have been better if I'd stayed away and sent a telegram saying: Congratulations.

(The Mother slaps Judith.)

MOTHER   You should be ashamed of yourself ...
(Silence)
If your father's a monster, she wasn't exactly a picture of innocence herself. She wasn't that stupid. She knew exactly how to manipulate him.

JUDITH   You're still defending him. All your life you've done nothing else but chant one refrain: Daddy's right. It's up to him. He knows what's best.

(The Mother begins to stack the plates.)

MOTHER   Why are you being so emotional? You were never particularly close to Anne. Perhaps when you were still children, but later you were ashamed of her. Did you ever go and visit her in the clinic? And now suddenly you've decided to champion her cause.
(She gets up.)

What your father did is wrong of course, but there are drives ...
which are stronger. You shouldn't get so worked up, for the sake
of the baby ... What's done is done. We mustn't lose sight of
reality. Your father is a very sick man. We must try to forget and
stop talking about it.

*(She walks wearily upstage, looks in the mirror and tidies her
hair.)*

SCENE 12

*Judith sits among the papers and reads. While the Mother remains
leaning against the mirror.*

JUDITH   'I'm twelve. I've got a ribbon in my hair, no breasts,
no pubic hair. Someone splashes water over my body with his
hands. The hands behave as if they have a sinister right to my
body. I tear myself free. I want to run away. I hear hideous
laughter. I run barefoot over the sand. I see him following me.
He's wearing a white suit with a rose in his lapel. He grabs my
pony tail and puts the end of it in his mouth. 'I could eat you up.
Yumm, I could eat up every last morsel of you.' His teeth are
yellow with silver at the back. I can see his dark-red tongue. He
throws me down near the tide mark. The water keeps coming
closer, waves with jagged white teeth. My body is stone. I
scream. Someone puts a hand over my mouth.
(Judith looks at her Mother.)
It was Mother.'
(The Mother doesn't react.)
'It was Mother. She shook me violently and said, Keep quiet or
you'll wake Judith ...'
MOTHER   She was always a strange child. She never reacted
the way you'd normally expect a child to. When we went to the
beach she walked along counting shells. She didn't even notice the
sea. She could never be where she was. When we were on a train
she pretended we were flying in an airplane. If we were on the

beach, we were in the desert. She always wanted to change the surroundings. I always had to use psychology on her. Whatever you say about your father, he was highly respected, especially at his work. And he saw to it that his children never wanted for anything. You could go to ballet lessons, tennis clubs ...

JUDITH   And I suppose I should be thankful to him for the rest of my days?

MOTHER   Every person has his good and bad qualities. When your child is born, will your painter boyfriend do the housework and help bring up baby? We'll have to see about that. Your father was a good breadwinner. You can't hold that against him. You can't say he wasn't a hard-working man.

(Silence.)

JUDITH   What do you think made him do it?
(No answer.)
Have you ever stopped to think about that? You told everyone she was psychotic, depressive. They all felt sorry for you and Daddy because fate palmed off a daughter on you who was such a failure. Have you ever tried to imagine what it's like to stand on a chair and fasten a rope around your neck? A rope you bought a few days before at a hardware store? Have you ever tried to imagine how desperate Anne must have been to kick the chair away from under her? And throw life into a black oblivion? The only life she had ...?
(She takes her Mother's hand.)
Come with me. I want to show you the hook she hanged herself from.

MOTHER   Are you trying to destroy me? Judith ...
(She pulls away.)
Maybe I made a mistake, but I did it out of love, love, love. When you're older you'll realise that you can't have it all your own way, that you have to bow your head and accept certain things.

JUDITH   What things? The Germans accepted that Hitler sent their sons to the front and we accepted that Jews were sent to the concentration camps and their children were gassed. Cowardice makes everything sordid. Cowardice ... Cowardice made you close your eyes to the most sordid and humiliating things in your life.

(The Mother exits and takes bags of clothing with her. Judith and the two chairs remain dimly lit.)

How could I have lived in this house for all those years, this hotbed of deceit? And what a show of pretence: Sunday walks with two adorable little daughters in white shoes, the ideal family. I must have been blind.

(Rock'n'roll music. Anne enters and begins to dance. Judith joins in. They dance facing each other. Their dancing becomes increasingly frenzied. Judith collapses from exhaustion. But Anne continues dancing. She starts beating her chest with her fists. It resembles a desperate self-castigation.)

SCENE 13

Anne is in the clinic. The Father, the Mother, Judith and Anne's school boyfriend are upstage on the raised platform. Anne is in the foreground. She is sitting on the floor surrounded by writing pads. The Psychiatrist is positioned between the two areas.

ANNE   Dear Judith. I miss you. I have nothing to give you, but I do miss you. I'm writing from the clinic. The window in my room looks out onto the park. There's a tree there, so old and big - if only you could take a photo of me coming out of the hollow trunk, like you did once before ...
(pause)
I remember that far-off place when we were children, the autumn trees burning on carpets of gold ... flash flash ... and we're back on the hill. Snow was falling ... but that was in the winter and you sat behind me on the sled. Your arms held me tightly as we whooshed down the slope in the cold, crystal-clear air ... flash flash ... and we're back in that long-lost world ... *(pause)*

But now I'm in this world, far away from you, and it's not real.
I'd like to call you, Judith. But I don't know your telephone
number and I don't dare to call home and ask for it.
(pause)
Yesterday they fastened black tubes to my head. They sent a
current of so many volts through them because they want to see
what's inside my brain. When I wash my hair I can still feel the
painful places where they fastened the tubes. They made me look
at a board with a black mark and a ball of light circling around it.
I'm not allowed to swallow and must try not to blink my eyes.
That sneaky ball looks into my brain ... What does it see there?
Does it see my fear? The therapists jump on every scrap of my
thoughts. Under their gaze I become a drop of water. I spread out
like an ink blot. They shout, 'Where are you? Where are you
hiding? You're not allowed to hide.'

SCENE 14

Anne begins walking around like a somnambulist.

ANNE   I feel so bad, so lonely, so lost, so wrong.
I need to hide underground ...
no room for my head ...
Don't deserve to breathe, don't deserve room to exist in -
in shallow land ...
please write-
in the wind ...
in the sand ...
in the nothing under the sea ...

PSYCHIATRIST Don't be frightened Anne. All I'm going to do is
help you feel calm. Hypnosis is a bridge to your unconscious.
We're going back to when you were a child. Would you like that,
Anne? Don't be frightened. You'll enter a twilight zone, but
you'll know what's happening. Your head will fall onto your
chest, very relaxed. You're breathing calmly. Your feet can feel

the ground and it's pleasurable. Now the journey is going downwards. Where are your feet taking you Anne?

ANNE   A swimming pool. The water sways to and fro, everything sways in my head and makes me nauseous. Underwater the steps of the ladder writhe. Like snakes.

PSYCHIATRIST Is there anyone near you?

ANNE   There are no other children. I'm alone. I see my own shadow swimming along with me on the azure bottom, the sunlight falls through the water, it shimmers deep below me on the tiles. My shadow is large and black and it rolls onto its back and has a white stomach. No, no, I don't want to.

Shark's teeth protrude from its lips. There's a shark trapped in the swimming pool with me. No, I don't want to ... He's got mean eyes.

PSYCHIATRIST Give me your hand. I'll pull you out of the water. Should we look at him, Anne? Should we look at the shark?

(Anne turns away.)

MOTHER   She's been like that since she was a child, scared of water, scared of the sea. She didn't even want to look at it. I put her in a deep deck chair because she liked it and said, 'Sit quietly and eat your sandwich.' From the deck chair she couldn't look to left or right, like a horse wearing blinkers. That forced her to look at the sea. I always had to use psychology on that child.

(Anne rests on her knees with her head on the floor.)

PSYCHIATRIST Don't try to hide. I know you're here. I want to talk to you.

ANNE   Questions, questions, your eyes are full of questions....

PSYCHIATRIST You have a beautiful body. Do you like it when men touch you?

(Anne doesn't answer.)

Do you know what love is? Don't you know? Surely everyone
wants to know that?

ANNE Everyone? Who are they?

MOTHER We gave her so much love. My husband doted on
her. He was always giving her presents; a toy panther, a little
suitcase, I remember a sky-blue woollen coat lined with milk-white
silk. Not very practical. Typical for a man to buy something like
that.

ANNE Love ... Peanut butter and blood.

PSYCHIATRIST I'm with you Anne. We'll go on together. We
must go back to the place where you remember everything. Just
let yourself go. Look around you. What do you see?

ANNE Do sharks have hands?

PSYCHIATRIST We've left the shark behind us, Anne. The
shark's trapped in the swimming pool. It can't live on dry land.

ANNE I've never been so tired It's hot here. Look, a wild,
white stinging nettle. It's covered with weeds here, wild stinging
weeds ... a false trail of stinging nettles. Stinging nettle juice is the
best way of inducing abortion.

*(She places her hands on her stomach as if she were pregnant.
She laughs. The Psychiatrist addresses the audience as if
delivering a lecture.)*

PSYCHIATRIST Neurotic symptoms don't always derive from
actual occurrences, but from wishful fantasies. Delusions of being
fondled and rape fantasies often play a major role. In some
mentally-disturbed women even being covered by bedclothes gives
rise to the illusion that someone's lying on top of them.
Hallucinatory sensations of the internal organs are related to this.
In Anne's case peristaltic movements are interpreted as the
movements of a child in her womb.

MOTHER She was always obsessed by babies. As a child she
had a macabre imagination. She drew embryos with daggers stuck
through them .... Later on she burnt those drawings in the garage.
She almost set the garage on fire ...

ANNE   I had two babies. But one of them was dead. It lay at the bottom of my stomach where I always have such a pain....

PSYCHIATRIST *(to audience)* Freud discovered that, as an embryo, every person was Oedipus, that the primal longing of the daughter was to conceive a child by her father. But everyone draws back in horror at the realisation of this wish and reacts by repressing it. This explains the dead child. The living and the dead baby indicate the discrepancy between the infantile and the present situation of the patient.

MOTHER   In the autumn of that year she started behaving strangely. She wouldn't get up in the mornings. She slept on long after my husband had left for work and Judith for school. Sometimes I found her wrapped in her old counterpane. She lay on the floor and had hidden herself under the bed. She wouldn't go to school for days on end. And then she would sit there writing as if possessed. She had to do a project about Kafka. She chose that peculiar story about the man who woke up one morning to discover he'd turned into a monstrous beetle. I read what she'd written and thought, 'Oh my god, that story will drive her completely mad.' I found her words so bizarre that I can remember them exactly - 'I feel like a beetle too,' she wrote. 'I crawl along the ceiling and see my body lying far below me. I crawl ... I crawl and I can't escape.'

PSYCHIATRIST The initial symptom of hysterical depression.

FATHER   Psychiatrists ... what good are they? They're busybodies. They stick their noses into other people's heads as if it was their god-given right. If these shrinks get at you they can make you believe anything. Depressed ... Have you any idea how many people in this world are depressed?

ANNE   Loneliness, who can bear it? To be alone with this secret, this darkness, following its course, regardless of my thoughts, my will power ... I hear voices in my head,
'You want it too, you're a *whore.*'
(pause)
Let it end. Let all the bad blood flow out of me so I can again be as innocent as I was when I was seven and laughed at squirrels

chasing each other in circles around a tree trunk. Is this what it all comes down to? Pain and peanut butter? Is it all illusion? The people, the houses, all an illusion? Is the tall grass in the backyard an illusion ....?

PSYCHIATRIST What's in the backyard, Anne?

(Anne lies crouched on the floor and doesn't react.)

You can't avoid your past. You can't strangle the child you once were and say, 'I want nothing to do with you.' No, an old self will seek revenge ... it'll become a kind of demon and will tyrannise you. We must go in search of that child ...'

SCENE 15

Her school boyfriend comes forward and joins Anne in the pool of light.

ANNE What's the time? My father gets home at six.

BOYFRIEND We've got plenty of time. What's the problem?

ANNE I don't want him to find you here. Not in the garden, not in the grass ...

BOYFRIEND Let's go up to your room then.

ANNE Not in my room ...

FATHER *(From the darkness upstage)* I wasn't born yesterday. Where did you meet that boy? Just by chance ... at the gym, just by chance ... on the tennis court, where do you meet boys? By chance, always by chance, but I followed you in the car this afternoon. I was thirty yards behind you. You didn't know that, did you? I saw you riding your bikes together, holding hands. Do you think it'll end there?

BOYFRIEND *(Takes her hand)* Your hands are so cold ...

ANNE Do you believe in life after death?

BOYFRIEND No, I don't. Do you?

ANNE Then I might as well die now.

BOYFRIEND Why do you talk that way? I've brought you something. It's not valuable. I mean it's not valuable to anyone

else, but it is to me. That's why I'm giving it to you. Maybe
you'll laugh at me.

ANNE   A stone ...

BOYFRIEND It's an onyx. It protects you against your enemies
and strengthens friendship.

ANNE   It's still warm ... from your hand.

BOYFRIEND What's that there?

(Anne pulls her arm away.)

On the inside of your arm? Blood ... Did you cut yourself?

ANNE   I scratched it on the thorns ... there are thorns
everywhere.

(She holds the stone up to the light.)

It's transparent, almost black.

Last night I dreamt about a black dove which flew into my room.
It sat on my shoulder, pressed up against me, here, between my
neck and my cheekbone, but suddenly it was a black rabbit and
was half-dead. Yes, it died, and instead of blood a white fluid
came pouring out.

BOYFRIEND Weird dreams ...

*(He tries to pulls her towards him, but she holds him at arm's
length.)*

ANNE   Do you think I look funny?

BOYFRIEND Hell no, you look great, with your hair like that ...
you crazy kid.

(Anne laughs and briefly moves up against him.)

ANNE   That's what my sister always says, ' crazy kid.' She
says there's nothing logical about me. I'm useless. Judith isn't.
She can make my mother laugh. I can't even do that ... Sometimes
I'm really scared. Not of weird guys or anything like that, but just
of fear itself ... I don't want to lose you, but I'm afraid I'm not
strong enough to hold onto you. My father doesn't want us to see
each other.

BOYFRIEND Can't you run away? Surely your father doesn't
decide what you do with your life? When we've finished school
we could go to America together ...

ANNE　　　It's pointless. I'm *useless*. I haven't felt like doing anything lately, except feeling miserable. I walk, watch, do things. Sometimes I can't even think in words.

BOYFRIEND I love you. You shouldn't worry so much. Try and have nice dreams every now and then. Not only ones about dying doves ... or was it a rabbit?

(Anne laughs. He draws her towards him. But Anne resists.)

ANNE　　　It's too hot ... everything prickles. My dress is sticking to my back ... I can't ...

BOYFRIEND I'm sweating too... what's the difference if we like each other?

(He grabs her. But she struggles skittishly.)

What are you scared of?

ANNE *(Trying to find words)* It's as if my body still feels something, but it can't get through to my brain ... as if there's a block in my neck ... Do you understand?

BOYFRIEND No, I don't understand. I don't go for all this psychology stuff.
(Discouraged, he lets go of her.)
You've got to want it yourself ...

ANNE　　　What do you mean by that?

BOYFRIEND You've got to want to believe in it　in us being together.
(Anne doesn't answer.)
Have you ever loved anyone? Like now ...?

ANNE　　　No, not like now.

BOYFRIEND Anyone else then? In a different way?

(Anne doesn't answer. He tries to kiss her again. Suddenly she slaps his face. He recoils and looks at her with pained incomprehension. Then he runs off.)

SCENE 16

Music: A thin electronic sound, reminiscent of the electro-shocks in Anne's head. In the course of the following monologue she begins to make movements as if scrubbing herself.

ANNE   I want to stand in icy water. I'm filthy. I'll never be clean again - I must purge my body with ice.
(She makes scrubbing movements.)
I must stand like this until all memory leaves me. A cold, pristine world around me, and the warm lips of the sun on my face ...
(She scrubs herself.)
But everything keeps coming back: all the ugliness, the brutal way he fingers me, down there between my legs, and in spite of everything my body responding with hot wetness as we do it behind the bolted door ... in the garage, in the basement ... while the nausea leaches to my skin with suction cups, and the never-ending hatred - for myself. I try to turn into stone. I feel my pain as a stone would.

(Anne tears a strip of material from her clothes and fastens it tightly around her breasts.)

PSYCHIATRIST Why are you doing that, Anne?
ANNE   They must go back. Back under my ribs. Back, back...
PSYCHIATRIST There's nothing wrong with your body. Why shouldn't you be proud of it?
ANNE   They're boils ... ugly boils. He says, 'You're going to have nice little tits.' They must go.
PSYCHIATRIST Who said that?
(Anne doesn't answer. She continues binding in her breasts.)
ANNE   They must go. The hands mustn't find them ...

(The Psychiatrist shows Anne her scissors. He has them in his pocket or finds them on the floor among her clothes.)

PSYCHIATRIST Do you recognise these?

ANNE   The scissors.

PSYCHIATRIST Why scissors?

ANNE   That pair of scissors is my friend. It cuts me open.

PSYCHIATRIST Do you want to punish your body?

ANNE   I enjoy the pain.

PSYCHIATRIST *(To audience)* Rejection of one's body, repression of sexual urges, can lead to aggressive behaviour. In hysterical patients one frequently sees how such aggression finds expression in a tendency towards castigation of the self or self-mutilation.

(Anne is still obsessively preoccupied with binding in her chest.)

ANNE   They must go ...

PSYCHIATRIST What are the hands doing? Whose body do the hands belong to?

ANNE   I can't see anything. There's a ... thick wad of cotton wool on my eyes.

PSYCHIATRIST Let's look at the hands. Can you see the hands? The face?

ANNE   There is no face.

PSYCHIATRIST I'll turn back the clock. We're going back in time. You are Anne and you're twelve years old.
(Anne walks around in the light.)
There's no-one here who wants to harm you. Go on. Go down the stairs, one step and then another, down, down. Where are you now?

ANNE   There are long corridors. With closed doors, lots of closed doors ... There's a tower full of cages. Everything's red.

PSYCHIATRIST Now we're going towards the red. I'll hold onto you.

(The Psychiatrist stands behind her. His hands caress her shoulders. He kisses her neck.)

ANNE   Hot waves go through me. I don't want to. No, I
said no ... It's red here and there are no windows, flame-coloured
and not a single window.

(As if in a trance, Anne recites a nursery rhyme.)

Dark red room
Is anybody home?
Father's there in the gloom
He's all on his own
Thief, thief, he sang
Tomorrow you will hang

ANNE *(shouting)* Mummy, Mummy ...

(The Mother leaps out of her chair and goes to Anne.)

SCENE 17

MOTHER   Quiet now ... What have you done to yourself, you
look awful? I can't be everywhere at once. I've got work to do.

*(She dresses Anne as if she were still a child. She puts on her
knee-length socks and a blue, woollen children's coat and ties a
ribbon in her hair.)*

There, that's better. You cause me so much trouble. You only
think of yourself ... You're not going to throw up now, are you?
Don't you dare. Not on your nice new coat.

*(The Mother leads Anne by the hand to the Father, as if she were
a little girl. She helps her onto his knee. Anne and the Father
remain.)*

ANNE   I must die, Daddy.
FATHER   You're crazy. Why must you die?

ANNE   I've been naughty.

FATHER   No, you haven't been naughty. You're Daddy's
precious little girl.

ANNE   Will I have to go to hell when I die?

FATHER   There's no hell. Nor any heaven. That's a lot of
nonsense. Who put that into your head? You mustn't listen to
what other people say. Just to me. If you listen to me I'll be nice
to you.

ANNE   Yes, Daddy.

FATHER *(Caressing the woollen coat)* My little kitten. When I put
you on the chamber pot at night you clung half asleep in my arms,
with your chubby claws around my neck. I could feel your small,
smooth thighs in my hand while you did a wee ... Then I let my
hands move upwards and I felt the moisture running over my
fingers, your eyes were drowsy with sleep, your hair stuck against
your forehead. Your face was as white as virgin snow on a
Sunday morning.

(He runs his hands along her coat.)

I had a kitten once. Just as soft as you ... I found it in a trash can.
I hid the cold little thing under my coat. I felt it getting warmer. It
dug its claws into my sweater and the pinpricks of pain in my chest
sent a wave of happiness through me: at last I had something that
was mine ... But my mother said, 'Take that filthy animal back to
where you found it. We can't keep a cat here.' I said, 'Mummy,
I'll look after him. He won't be a nuisance ...' 'Alright', she said,
'you can feed the cat in the shed, but he's not allowed to come
into the house ...' 'Not even at night?' I asked. 'Never', she said,
'a cat outside or no cat at all ...' I put the cat in a box and locked
him in the shed. I called him Panther. I dreamt he would become
big and strong and terrorise the whole neighbourhood at night.
He'd only listen to me. I learnt his language, because that's how
you get along with animals. I miaowed and hissed at him and he
hissed back with his baby mouth opened wide, ha ha....

(pause)

One day my father said, 'What's that I hear in the cupboard? Is
that dirty animal in here? God help you if you're lying ...' I said,

I'm sorry, Daddy, I'll get him out ...' 'Is he in there?' My mother
shouted, 'Is he in there pissing in my shoes?' My father grabbed a
stick and I started pleading, 'Don't do it, Daddy ...' But he tore
open the cupboard and started lashing out in every direction. If
only it was a real panther, I thought, but the terrified little animal
shot up the wall like a bullet and clung to the curtains ... Suddenly
there was a sharp squeal and my kitten dropped to the floor. I
could see his legs buckling under him as he tried to escape and the
fur on his head was stuck together in a dark wet patch. My father
grabbed him by his neck and threw my kitten out of the window.
'Not to worry', he said, 'a cat always lands on its feet.'

Yes ... My father was a hard man. Whenever he saw boys fighting
in our street, he boxed my ears until I was gasping for breath and
said, 'Go on, take those boys on. You're not a nancy-boy, are
you?'
(pause)
It didn't kill me, but it made me strong.

*(During this speech Anne has slid off his knees and onto the
floor, where she leans against the wheelchair. The Father runs
his fingers through Anne's hair.)*

Your hair is darker than it used to be ... And you've cut it short.
(Querulous.)
You know how I like you with long hair. Are you crying about the
cat? Just think, pain can never be worse than when you hold your
hand on a hot plate. There's a limit to pain ...

SCENE 18

*Anne gets up, walks to the children's chairs where she removes her
coat and the ribbon from her hair. She walks back to her Father as
a mature young woman.*

FATHER   So you've come back. Maybe you thought I'd kick
the bucket. Maybe you were hoping that's happen, but there's
still life in this tough old carcass. Feel the strength in my hands...
*(Anne doesn't move. He reaches out his hands and suddenly
speaks obsequiously and emotionally.)*
Anne ...

ANNE   Father ...
(She lets him take her hand.)
You're holding my hand. Why? Oh, I get it ... you don't have to
pretend. But now you'll have to meet my conditions. Now *I'm* the
night snake, Father.

FATHER   What conditions? Oh, you mean that ... I don't even
know if I'd feel like it.
(Looks at her critically.)
You've not got any prettier. You're so skinny. Didn't they give
you enough to eat in that loony bin? And that dress ... It's just a
rag.

ANNE   And you? You still think you're god's gift to women.
Mother says you piss in your pants.
(She pulls her hand away, smiles.)
You crippled old toad.

FATHER   Still my thoroughbred pony ... Rearing up.

ANNE   I wanted to kill you ... Did you know that? With your
own razor. But now I know it's pointless, because even if you
were dead your face would always loom up in front of me. I see
your image reflected in the eyes of every man who looks at me.
Every man who wants anything from me is you. You are in my bed
every night, in my dreams, my nightmares - there you are, in
disguise, but the horror is still the same...Did you think I was too
small to feel anything? Did you think my flesh wouldn't
remember...? I was your possession. Never a person.
(Silence.)
After all these years I wish I could say, my feelings for you are
dead. I wish I could feel like I'd never had a father.

FATHER   Anne, don't talk like that. I thought you'd come back
because you still felt something for me ... because of what we had

together. Things were fine between us when you were small. You climbed into my bed in your nightdress and snuggled up in my arms ... Come here, my girl.

ANNE   If I could forgive you, perhaps I'd be free ... If I could walk right through you, through the smiling phantom you are and leave you behind like something that means absolutely nothing to me anymore, maybe then I could breathe, laugh and begin a new life ... but I wouldn't know how to forgive you.

(Anne bends over him and kisses him on his forehead.)

Take care of yourself, Father.

(Anne exits.)

SCENE 19

The stage is as in the First Act. Light comes on above Judith sitting among the papers. Perhaps she's sitting on the floor now or in Anne's rocking-chair.

JUDITH   Now I know everything. I can see your lives stripped naked. Like the old tree we pulled the bark off and under that were white larvae, pale bodies growing in obscurity, writhing, shunning the light, revolting.
And I saw nothing, understood nothing. When I think of you now lying in the earth ... We're sisters, you said, we carry the same scars ...

(She lays her hand on her stomach. To the child.)

What should I hope for? That you're a boy? Not if you're like him. But if you're a girl, a little woman, I'll be your ally - I'll teach you to trust no-one, no single man, not even your own father... What a god-awful world where no-one can be trusted.

(Judith walks to the Father. He's playing chess, as he was at the beginning of the play.)

FATHER The pawns in closed ranks ... from the left flank. My bishop to C-4 ...

(The Father sees Judith.)

So you're coming to see how it's going with the old man? I thought you'd be busy tidying up the house.

(He looks at her appreciatively.)

Being pregnant suits you. You've become a beautiful woman. I'd walk past you on the street without even recognising you.

JUDITH I want to talk to you.

FATHER I'm at your mercy. Where could I go? I'm stuck here like a rabbit in a snare. Wouldn't you like to pour your sick old Dad a drink first? *(Judith pours whisky for both of them.)*

JUDITH I look at you. I know you and I don't know you. Just a face with *Father* stuck on it.

FATHER What have you got to say? Get it off your chest.

JUDITH I'm going to ask you something, although I know you're going to lie to me.

FATHER It sounds as if you're going to file a complaint.

JUDITH Did you go to bed with your own daughter, for years on end? From the time she was a little child?

FATHER What put that idea into your head? What are you insinuating?

JUDITH I'm going to read something to you.

(She unfolds a piece of paper.)

'On my twelfth birthday Daddy gave me a toy panther, a suitcase... *(Judith looks at her Father.)* and a diaphragm. He said, Now you're becoming a woman.'

It's Anne's handwriting.

FATHER She must have been joking? Using a big word without knowing the exact meaning.

(Silence)

Maybe she used one of those things when she was sixteen and hung around with that boy?

JUDITH   No. I saw you together, you and Anne in the big bed
when Mother was in hospital.

FATHER   I can't believe you'd dare to make such an accus-
ation. Against your own father.

JUDITH   I've got a right to know certain things.

FATHER   What do you take me for, Judith?

JUDITH   That's the question I'm putting to my father.

FATHER   You talk as if I was a criminal.

JUDITH   Right now I could almost believe you're what you
seem to be - a helpless old man. The whole room stinks of piss
and disinfectant. Decay ... But you keep smiling that false smile of
yours, the one you used to get ahead in the world, the one you
used to seduce Mummy with, when you were a married man.

FATHER   I never made a secret of the fact I was married, but oh
no, she was prepared to settle for a small part of me rather than
nothing at all. She's the one who wouldn't give up. There were
these two women who both depended on me for support. Going
through that divorce wasn't easy for me. I felt I was a failure, a
traitor. By the way, seeing we're bringing everything out into the
open - your mother had been fooling around quite a bit before she
picked up with me ... Who says Anne was mine?
(Silence.)

JUDITH   You're lying ... Mother was still a virgin.

FATHER *(shrugs his shoulders.)*   There was no certificate
pinned on Anne's chest when she was born.

JUDITH *(Confused)* Are you trying to tell me she wasn't your
daughter? Or are you just saying that because it suits you?

FATHER   Your mother had been to a convent school. She
seemed naive, but meanwhile .... You know what those Catholics
are like. Why do we have to dig all this up?

JUDITH   Why did you marry her then? It's all so sordid,
sordid ...

FATHER *(softly)* Because I loved her. She wasn't much more than
a child. She had to fend for herself. Her mother had remarried a
German and was living in Cologne. One day she phoned me at the
office in a panic because she was desperately sick.

JUDITH   And so you crawled into her bed to comfort her?

FATHER   Feelings are one thing and sex is another. Some
people lean more towards sex and others more towards feelings.
Women are always going on about 'feelings', but when they're out
to catch a man ...   *(He holds up his glass for more whisky.)*

JUDITH   Oh, I hate you. I hate both of you.
(She draws back from him and becomes increasingly emotional.)
There you sat on your throne - you were always going on about
respectability, you criticised everyone, you thought you were so
superior. But you never had the faintest idea of what was going on
inside other people. You weren't interested ... What was going on
inside Anne ... You used her like a doll, a lifeless doll. And you're
still sitting there without flinching ... Oh, you make me want to
puke.

(Mother enters.)

MOTHER   Have you been giving your father whisky Judith?
You know it's not good for him.
(She removes the whisky bottle. The Father points to his wife.)

FATHER   I stopped drinking for her sake. I had to be an ideal
husband. I worked hard. I asked nothing for myself ...
(Judith walks to the telephone.)

JUDITH   I'm getting out of here right now.
(Nervously she dials a number. No answer.)

FATHER   Not at home? Maybe this boyfriend of yours has got
a girlie tucked away somewhere, who poses for him. After all,
artists need a model and you can hardly pose for him with that fat
stomach. You're going to be a *mother*. A devoted mother, just
like that one over there who suffocates a man with maternal care.

JUDITH   Why am I wasting my energy on such worthless
people?   *(She cries.)*

MOTHER   You're upset. It's because of your condition. Every
family has its ups and downs.

JUDITH   You call this *ups and downs*?   *(Calmer now.)*
I've told him that I know about his relationship with Anne.

(Mother sits down on a chair as if she's deadbeat.)
(Silence.)

I'm facing something I've got no words for.

(Looks at her Mother.)

And you didn't protect her against him.

FATHER *(to Mother)* I told her to let it be and not to stir things up. But she's behaving like a self-appointed examining magistrate.

(Silence.)

Let's say something did happen ... Things like that are very natural ... a human impulse. Today they've discovered that children themselves want it. It's no longer taboo. Our society condemns it, but in other societies it's more or less acceptable. Take Gandhi for example, who in later life preached chastity ... that man used to go to bed with his own daughters and granddaughters. You didn't know that, did you? No-one took offence. A man simply needs more sex than he can get from any one woman.

MOTHER   So Anne was just what you needed. Apparently I was no longer good enough for you.

FATHER   Would you have preferred me to go to a whore?

MOTHER   A whore ... you were dead scared of whores, scared of catching something.

FATHER   I didn't want to hurt your feelings. You were always so worried about your good name ... No, I can't see anything wrong with it. I only wanted to make Anne happy. She asked for it.

MOTHER   You didn't have to prove yourself to her ... is that it?

JUDITH   Anne is *dead* ... and you two only talk about yourselves.

MOTHER   He didn't love her. He's incapable of loving anyone besides himself.   *(She holds her handkerchief to her mouth.)*

FATHER   You're hard. Everyone who puts a foot wrong is forgiven in the end, but not me. We all need a little understanding, a little sympathy. But you don't know the first thing about that. *(He looks at Judith.)* You're just as narrow-minded as your mother.

(Judith throws her drink in his face. The Father takes his handkerchief out of his pocket and painstakingly starts drying his face.)

MOTHER I haven't got the strength any longer to sympathise with everyone. I've suffered enough. *(She cries.)*

FATHER That's the one thing you women are good at - suffering. You try to outdo each other at it. People who suffer always think they're in the right. Victims are always entitled to pity ... You're in a strong position when you suffer and you women know exactly how to manipulate us with your eternal suffering.
(Judith and her Mother walk away from him. Judith supports her.)
Go on then, go and think up ways of how to do me in. But just don't think I'll put an end to my own life.

JUDITH Everything comes to an end.

(Father clutches the armrests of the wheelchair.)

FATHER I won't let myself be beaten. I've always fought my way through. Through the war, through hard times ...
(The Father attempts to rise out of his chair. He sways and falls, mumbling with a hand in front of his eyes.)
I won't resist ... I won't resist any longer. Anne ... I'm a monster, a despicable person ... Your face is a white blur ... like ash.
(He drags himself across the floor.)
Make a hole in the wall. I can't breathe.

(The Mother hears the fall - or perhaps he knocked over the table and computer when he fell - in any event, she comes running.)

MOTHER *(Calling)* Judith, your father has fallen over.
(She tries to pull him up.)
Try and get up, Louis.
(The Father doesn't answer. The Mother shakes him to and fro.)

Say something to me ... It's me, Linda, your wife.

JUDITH   He's shamming.

FATHER   I'm dying.

MOTHER   You're not dying. I don't want you to die. I just want you to forgive me. I've forgiven you so often. All my life. Forgive me now, after this terrible day.

FATHER   When will all this torment end ...?

(Judith has entered and motionlessly observes these two people, her parents.)

MOTHER *(To Judith)* It's all your fault. How could you carry on like that in front of a sick man?

(Judith bends over with her hand in front of her mouth. The Mother raises the Father back into his chair.)

(Lighting change. Spot on Judith alone.)

JUDITH   I no longer have a home.

(Lights.)

Inez van Dullemen

Inez worked briefly as a speech therapist, taught acting and worked with her partner Erik Vos, the director on various projects for *Appeltheater*. She began writing short stories, novels and travelogues for magazines and newspapers before turning to playwriting. Travel has been the focus of her life and work, including the inner journey to other people's dreams and fears and the outer journey to other countries, people and threatened cultures.

She has been awarded prizes for her journalism and fiction and in 1989 the Anna Bijns prize for her contribution to literature.

THE CARACAL

by Judith Herzberg
translated by Rina Vergano

THE CARACAL was first performed in Dutch in January 1988 in Theater Bellevue in Amsterdam, the Netherlands.
The text was written in collaboration with Motti Averbuch.

Woman   Marjon Brandsma

Director   Gerardjan Rijnders

A monologue. Evening.
Woman of around 30-40 years old alone in a room. She is speaking on the telephone.

WOMAN   Listen.

What for

And if you had it in black and white, what good would it do you?

What do you mean?

I said right from the start: till the end of the year.

I'm not dropping it 'just like that'.

You're not letting me finish.

I *did*. Christ, I'm sitting here apologising about what I do feel and don't feel as if -

but you said yourself: six months is better than nothing
how was I supposed to know?

No I don't feel like another crime film.

No I don't feel like a nice meal.

That's right, I do feel too good for that.
I've been fasting for a couple of days.

Because.

Distance. From food, from you, from everything, yes.

So you'll have it in writing. Old fashioned.

Why not have me on video? Young as I am today, forever.

Sometimes you just know. I feel that I'm going to change very
quickly, very suddenly and completely

that too yes

That I really loved you?
? ? ?

(Silence)

If you can explain to me what that is.

No not now, really not. I want to be left in peace.

In peace! I need to think, I need to think it through myself too.

The caracal?

Yours?

What do you mean the caracal is yours
I don't remember a thing about it.

The first night? Did I give it to you then? I don't remember.

Yes extremely shallow.

During the daytime. I spend my days dealing with that, with
reality.
(Furious outburst on the other end of the line.)
Stop it! Stop it! Shut up!

Okay, then I'm spiteful.

Okay, then I'm untrustworthy.

I said from the start: till the end of the year,

and if I gave it to you, then come and get it.
But not now!
I swear it! Straight after the holiday if you must, but not now,
not for this one week! *(Hangs up.)*

(Telephone rings. She jumps. Answers it.)

Yes,

Vera.

yes, fine.

right. Nice of you to call. How are things?

I don't even have a moment to think of *myself.*

Yes, work, busy, you know. The school, parents, children -

Come again? New Year's Eve? Why? Are you alone?

Vera, you know I don't believe in that kind of thing.

I always used to say to mother -

What?

(A different, suddenly sharp voice.)
What did you say? Can you say that again?

'Watch out for the caracal?' Did she say that? 'For the caracal?'
did she say that?
What did she mean by that, I mean, what on earth? *(Laughs)*
Because I was just talking to someone about a caracal.

When?

Last night?

Who else was there? Mrs Borodon-Shapira?
Who's that?

No, never heard of her.

Oh, the medium. Oh yes. I remember now. The dark one, with
the moustache. Is that the one?

Vera, you know perfectly well I love you dearly, but this sort of thing is just superstition.

She said that? That I should be careful I don't lose my pearl? What does she mean, my pearl?

Pearl stands for *what?*

(Laughs) But New Year's Eve that's a problem. I was looking forward to an evening at home by myself for once.

Whoever I want?

Yes, Mia, but she won't be able to of course.

What hasn't she got?

A metaphysical instinct? Have I got one then?

Just like mother?

Vera, it's very sweet of you, really, but I'll have to think it over.

Did she say that? Right fine. I'll call you. Bye.

Bye, bye, bye, bye.

Yes, of course I love you.

Bye, bye. *(Rings off, but doesn't hang up, immediately dials another number)*

Mia?

Oh, Katey. Poppet, is mummy at home?

Is she asleep?

Already.
(Corrects)
Still?
(Corrects)
Already?

No, it's nothing special.

No, don't wake her up.

Oh, is she up anyway?
How are you darling?

Kevin? The one with the ears? That's nice.

Yes, let me - (speak to mummy)

Mia. Sorry. I didn't know -

Yes, Vera just rang.

Vera Janowitz, Dr Janowitz wife, you know, those theosophists of mummy's.

She wants me to spend New Year's Eve at her place.
(Silence)
With you? It hasn't got anything to do with you.

But Mia, she said -

You know I don't believe in that kind of thing, but how could she have known that I'd broken it off with Alex? She phoned straight afterwards.

What do you mean, I shouldn't have?

No this time it's for good.

No it's not at all a shame that you never met him. That was deliberate. I knew it wouldn't last long. He kept wanting to meet my beautiful sister, but I didn't want him to.

Yes, and then I'd be running into yet another of my ex's at one of your parties, I'm not at all keen on that collection of yours.

Yes, if I want to I'll make my *own* appointments with them, one at a time, and not all together.

Yes, that's true, I'm sorry.

I told *him* I don't want to see him again.

He wants the caracal.

Yes, he knows exactly how attached I am to it. He does.

And suddenly Vera phones up and says that mummy appeared to

them yesterday at the seance and that she told Vera to warn me about the caracal. That's incredible isn't it? And she wants me to go to her for New Year. What shall I do?

You can't do that if someone's clairvoyant!
But what are your plans?

Oh yes. One more thing. If you donate any more clothes to those people, sew the buttons back on and take the stains out, because those people are asphyxiating on dirty ripped up clothes. They never have anything good, that's the point. They're choking on rubbish! Goodbye.

(Immediately dials another number. Light, flirtatious tone.)
Robert, sorry to call so late.

It's me.

It's me!

Can't you tell from my voice?

I wanted to make an appointment.

Me!

What do you mean 'so many me's'. There's only one me and that's me. You still don't know?
They're all so egocentric, are they? Incredible.

No that's an insult. Linda? No. I don't know who Linda is but she's not me. I'm sure Linda's very beautiful.

No, stop it, please, you're just making it worse.

Oh you're so cautious. No I'm not saying now, certainly not.

Then just put: 'mysterious voice', and wait and see.

Cut, wash, dry, perm, colour, everything.
How long will that take?

No, Thursday.

You're fully booked Thursday? But it's only Monday, that's why

I'm phoning *now*.

Yes, I can see that, but what with it being New Year's Eve -

No I *am* going out

But how do you know -

God that's mean, what a tease -

When?

Yes, I do make the odd call.

The whole evening that's nonsense.

Yesterday? What time?

Yes, I was on the phone then, that's right.

The day before yesterday. I can't remember, but it certainly wasn't the whole evening.

It's handy, the telephone. I don't have to leave the house.

And so what if I do! You sound just like a jealous lover or something.

What was it you wanted?

No, I don't take taxis any more

Those drivers.

Yes, and if they *don't* start coming on I'm insulted as well!
Do you know what happened? I had one who started off: 'And what kind of work do you do?' 'Guess,' I said. And do you know what he said?

Exactly!

Yes, but I don't *look* like a school teacher, do I?

Well then you're to blame. That's your frumpiness. Real headmistresses have creative hairdressers, who make them look -

no, go and answer it then.

No you don't have to, alright then ring, no I'll ring you back.
Bye!
(She hangs up, the phone rings immediately, she jumps.)

(Very businesslike) Yes, speaking.

No, if it's urgent. I do get called at home now and then.
About whom?

Oh yes.

Yes, I don't have the list here but I know who it is, very well.

Husky voice, always walks on his toes.
What? By his mother? It's usually the fathers who do the hitting.

Oh, he only hits the mother.
So the mother hits the boy.

What about the boy?

He doesn't hit anyone?

What does he do?

Kissing?

No of course we don't allow that. *(Laughs heartily)* I'm sorry.
(about the laughing)

Rather remarkable indeed. Who told you?

A lot of girls?

Yes, if four have complained then there must have been more.
He'll have to stop that, of course. Where does he get it from?

Well you're the psychologist. I've never heard anything like it.
How fortunate you're there. I wouldn't know how to handle that
kind of thing. I can't very well pin up a notice in the corridor:
'girls beware of the satchel piddler'. *(Laughs)*

No I don't think it's funny, not at all.

Of course it's a symptom. Urinating in satchels, that's a new one
on me.

If they came from normal families they wouldn't need us, although I do wonder if such a thing exists.

A normal family.

Criminal? Could be.

But why are you calling me this evening at home?

Yes of course it's shocking.

Why the father? I think both parents need to be talked to.

Have him taken away from them, I think that's going a bit too far.

Yes, I know him, he's called Jack.

Yes, I know him fairly well, from the P.T.A.

By fairly well I mean -

Yes, yes that's true, about two months ago, after a P.T.A. meeting, how do *you* know that?

He's mad!

He wouldn't do that.

it wasn't a relationship, just a few -

Bloody hell, that's none of anyone's business, I mean we didn't do it in the playground

Yes you do that

Yes that would be very sensible

Yes if you want his wife to know

Yes if you want a scandal on your hands

of course, I'd have to accept dismissal, but you should ask yourself whose interests you would be serving. Goodnight.

What did you say? My libido fixated on criminal types?

God almighty!

Kind? Kind? Is that psychology? Your own kind?

God almighty!

(Puts the telephone down, but doesn't ring off. We can possibly hear someone continuing to talk on the other end. She picks up the receiver and listens to see if they're still talking, puts it down again, listens again. The person on the other end has apparently hung up. Now she hangs up as well, pats the telephone on the shoulders and says:)
It's not your fault. You're innocent.
(Dials)
Vera?

It's a real bore, but straight after I spoke to you I got this call from the airport from an old friend. He's over for a couple of days and the only time he's free is the evening of the thirty-first. I haven't seen him for years.

Yes Australia, how do you know?

Incredible. How long it's been? Seven years or so.

What, nine years and five months, how do you know that?

I'll ask. I'll ask him when he left exactly, and I'll let you know, alright?

Bye, darling, see you very soon, got to hang up, bye, bye.
(Dials)
Robert, what's going on, why don't you phone? Robert I'm at my wits end.

No not over the telephone, it's not for the telephone.

No I don't want you to come

no please don't

no I can't go out

no that's silly

never mind, leave it, I'm a bit confused.
(Laughs) Yes, bye darling, bye. Robert? I'm so frightened that they're going to come and murder me.

No I don't think it's a turn on at all

no I'm really frightened

what kind of shady characters

that's not true Robert, no it's not a joke

certainly not

yes, Thursday *(Hangs up.)*
Thursday.

(Telephone rings.)
Mia, darling, I can't talk for long. I've been waiting for a call the whole evening.

No just a local call, but I'm being phoned constantly about other things, I'm constantly engaged and that's -

no go on, what is it

no, what is it?

alright I will, but it might be quite late.

I just got a call from the school psychologist.

A boy who pees in girls' satchels.

no you think everything's funny

because I had a fling with the father. Can you believe that?

Well I can't either, but she says he's going to put a knife into me.

You don't know him.

You don't know the man

what do you mean *kind* of man, that word drives me mad: *kind* of man!

He's simply a man

no not a simple man.

Why?

Do you really want to know why?

Because he had such beautiful arms, and because I really felt like having them round me, is that such an inconceivably strange idea?

Because I never tell you anything. It's only ever about you.

You never want to hear anything.

You're so full of your own nonsense, you only want me to tell you nice things. That jam you made - I threw it away. It went all mouldy. It could have exploded in the cupboard!

And why do I always have to hear everything about Simon and the children, it's my turn for once, I've never told you one single thing! Not one single thing!

Like how I feel when I come home on Wednesdays and have to open all the windows front and back to get rid of the sweaty smell of that professor of yours.

Do you really think Simon doesn't know about it? Mia? Mia? Mia?
(Other end has hung up. She sits still for a while, there is a growing tension between her and the telephone. She lays her head on the telephone. The telephone rings, she jumps.)

Who? Who do you want to speak to?

Dixon's the chemist? No.

Yes, that's the right number. But this is an ordinary house. This number's in the paper?

Late night chemist? Could you repeat the number?

I'm very sorry. I can't help you. I take it it's urgent.

Insulin? Why don't you go to casualty

For two hours? The bastards.

Your mother?

You don't need to tell me.

I've been through exactly the same thing. I hope not for her sake. My mother had diabetes for years. But she died of goitre in the end. All because of the drugs. You have to be so damn careful. Oh they prescribe them, they do that. But you don't know if they help or if they just make it worse. My mother only started to feel better when she stopped taking anything. The drugs I mean. But of course I don't know how far your - (mother)

yes, that's the worst of it.

Yes, during the night. In the end she had to give in to it, just be sick.

Yes

yes

Yes

that's right. Exactly.

How did you know?

Headmistress of a remedial school. A school for children with serious learning and behavioural problems.

You sound quite young

That *is* young. What do you do for a living, if you don't mind my asking?

What?

Oh really? That's another field entirely Where is that?

What kind of people?

No. I'm no good in -

yes I'm sure it's interesting. A sort of club, something like that?

No I never go out. You know what it's like with a family. You never have time for anything. Yes three children. A husband, two dogs. But is there anything I can do for you?

Shall I try and look up the number of the chemist for you?

Yes, just give me your number. If I can find it, I'll call you.
(Searching for a pencil and paper.)

Yes, yes, I've got one, go ahead.

641 3741. That's a nice easy number 641 3741. I'll -

Baz

Is that your name? Nice. Cheeky. Right. Okay. I'll call you back in a couple of minutes.

Don't mention it. It's the least I can do.

Perhaps you didn't call the wrong number after all - *(Laughs)*

Yes, yes, ta-ta.
(Hangs up, dials number.)

Hello, could you give me the number of Dixon's the chemist?

Yes Dixon's the chemist.

What did you say?

No chemist with that name.

No, not Dickens.

Do you perhaps know which chemist is open late this evening?

Yes, it's very urgent.

Galloway's? 661 4891.

Are you sure?

No, because it said something else in the paper.

This *is* from the paper? Thank you.

Thank you very much
(Hangs up, dials, muttering 641 3741)

Baz? It's not Dixon's it's Galloway's. 661 4891. Are you writing it down?

What?

What?

When?

No. God, how awful, how awful. Oh that's really awful. Can I do anything?

Of course.

Come over?

Over where? Now? But -

Come and get me? But we don't know each -

I can't just -

no you can't say that. Of course I want to help. But -

yes I do understand! But what can I do about it?

What? Blow job?

What did you say? Filthy bastard! Pervert! Everyone's sick. How dare you speak to me like that! I don't even know you! I'll call the police! *(Hangs up.)*
(Puts her hands over her eyes.)
(The telephone rings. She is frightened. She finally answers it, screams:)
Filthy bastard! Cheat! *(Stops)*
Vera?

What do you want? Sorry. I've just -

What did you say? I can't talk to you now. Please.

What did you say? You had a funny feeling I was in danger?

What do you mean 'danger'?

Why do you frighten me like this? I don't want to hear it. Not now.

Do what?

What?

Breathe out?

Blow the poison out? *(Breathes in and out.)*

Hold it?

Oh. *(Holds her breath, then breathes out again.)*

Like that?

Is that okay?

Do what?

The tip of my nose?

Yes, I'm looking at the tip of my nose.

No no, I won't say another word.
(Breathes)
(Breathes)

Yes, slightly dizzy.

Yes it's alright.

Falling asleep.

Yes, I understand.

Let my body sway along?

No, I haven't got my eyes shut.

No I won't say anything, I won't say another word.
(Silence)

Consciousness.
(Silence)
Centre.

(Silence)
The pearl.

(Silence)
Focus.

(Silence)

Empty myself, how?

From within?

(Silence)

Down to the minutest detail.

Yes, I understand.

Yes I understand. I can feel it. *(Breathes again)*

Wonderful. I feel completely different.

Honestly, Vera. Thank you.

No no yes yes, I'll come in any case.

Now I know -

What?

Vera just let me -

Vera, there was no Australian, nobody from Australia.

What do you mean, there *has* to be an Australian? I just made him up.

It doesn't make any difference? Oh that's what you mean.

Alright. I promise I'll go to sleep now.

Alright Vera. Bye, bye

Bye, bye, see you soon Goodnight.

(Dials)

Mia? Sorry. Everything's glass.

I said: everything's glass.

You don't understand? You do understand. I'm not going to explain it, but I love you. Aren't you angry with me any more? I want to tell you something, why I behave the way I behave -

Oh really? Oh, I thought I was usually much calmer. I'm in love. I love somebody.

For a year already

He *was* married when I met him

I don't know

three days

no three *days*, no nights

He was nice, nicer than I thought possible

yes and he thought I was nice, and beautiful. Are you really not angry with me any more? He really thought I was beautiful, that's so wonderful, to really be beautiful for once

of course it's important. How would *you* know -

No of course I haven't got club feet but I also wasn't born with a natural charm which I just happened to be blessed with and which made every single thing in my life ten times easier than it is for someone else.

Yes of course I mean you.

I don't begrudge it you, I just think that you should realise that you were born with it and that you shouldn't be so bloody satisfied with everything.

No? What for instance?

But even your junk is 'nice junk'. My junk is just rubbish.

Did he say that? The bastard. You're saying that because you're still angry about just now. You don't *have* to tell me that, do you? You're just ruining it for yourself!

It's not a compliment at all, and you know it. 'Bloodless' can never be a compliment no matter how often you put 'perfection' or 'perfect order' after it.

Alright in front of it then.

'Bloodless perfect order' is exactly the same as 'perfect but bloodless order.' If that's what he thinks then I never want him fucking you in my bed again.

That's off then, finished. Tell him to put that in his pipe-
What do you mean, arranged?

then phone him and tell him it's off.

So he's going to turn up on my doorstep on New Year's Eve?
But that's impossible, how can you possibly get away?

Switzerland? And you're not going with - just so you can spend
one night with that prat!

Well you can't because I'm not *going* to Vera's. I'm staying at
home with a good book and a bottle of wine.

Listen darling, just because you've got a husband and three
children and two slavering dogs and a job at the university doesn't
mean you have the right to commandeer me and my bedroom
whenever it suits you!

Well you could have just *asked* before making arrangements with
that professor of yours. I've told Vera I'm not coming now.

Oh, so Simon thinks you're spending a cosy New Year's Eve
with me does he?

Oh, you think he'll phone you, and then you'll have to be here.
And what it you're not here? And by the way it would have been
very nice if you had come to me for once, instead of me always
having to come to you.

Your cosy get-togethers make me sick and I shall be spending
December the thirty-first at home.

And if you want to hang up then hang up. I've become quite
immune to it this evening. *(Hangs up.)*

(Telephone rings.)

Stupid bitch? Who do you think you're calling a stupid bitch?
You stupid bastard. If you had any balls you wouldn't have
opened your mouth to that psychologist. What's it got to do with

her? Now everyone's going to find out, Mary too and then what?
That was the most stupid thing you could have done!

(Visibly startled) What do you mean gone?

Where have you looked?

And he wasn't there? No he hasn't been here.

Phoned? The phone's been engaged the whole evening.

No I don't think he's gone that far.

I think I know where he is.

I can't say. I swore I wouldn't tell.

How do I know? I often go round there for a can of tea.

yes, a can of tea

but it's very late now

I'll tell you, but on two conditions, Jack. One, that you don't call
me a stupid bitch. Two, that you don't smash the place up,
whatever you find there. Promise? Whatever you find there,
however bad it is?

Yes, that's why, that's precisely why I'm going to tell you,
because he shouldn't be there so late in the evening, he's much
too small for that. It's fine during the day. On your word of
honour?

And will you call me as soon as you've found him? Jack?
Promise?

You shouldn't get so worked up about it, that peeing in satchels.
They often do that at that age. It'll put itself right, I promise you.

at the back of the bike shed, if you walk right through to the back,
there's a wooden panel, up against the embankment, well you can
open it

yes, its dug out, it's dug into the embankment

call me when you've found him.

(Dials) Robert, angel, do you want to be in a film? Then you have to come with me New Year's Eve.

Someone they're going to make a film about. A friend of my mother's, she's older than my mother would have been, with supernatural powers and those little curls tight against her head and a moustache with pomade in it, I think she must be really proud of that moustache because she rubs pomade into it or did I already say that, and then she twists it into little twirls. But I don't know if I'm going myself yet, I've spent the whole evening, I've spent the whole week waiting for a telephone call and I can't bear it if it doesn't ring, so then I keep phoning people because I'm just sitting waiting, but actually I've been waiting a whole year Robert.

Well it's like this. Have you really got time? It's a long story.

In love for the first time, a year ago.
Married of course. Bad marriage etcetera. Crazy about me, head over heels, wants a divorce, promises, pleads, etcetera. I say no it's not my scene, in a year's time if you're divorced give me a ring, in the meantime no contact. Not see each other, not phone nor write. That's a year ago and that's why I'm sitting by the phone like an idiot.

Cancel all my appointments, get the sack, get murdered, I don't care as long as he phones. I can't stand it any more Robert.

Maybe they are back together again. Maybe he's dead. Maybe he's got divorced and married someone else in the meantime. I really don't know but I can't stand it any more. True love for the first time in my life. A whole year -

yes in my head, in my head I've been as faithful as a dog. What shall I do Robert, I can't stand it any more.

That's a good question.
(Ponders)
That I could finally stop postponing everything, that everything would stop being so makeshift all the time.

No, I'm not going to do that. I've stuck if out for a whole year so
I'm hardly going to turn round at the last minute and call *him*.
You wouldn't do that either.

you would, after half-an-hour

but if you'd controlled yourself every day for a *whole* year then
you wouldn't go and spoil it all at the last minute, would you?

Well *I* wouldn't

I'm not moralistic, I just don't want something like that on my
conscience. Sleep tight darling.
I'm staying up a bit longer. *(Hangs up)*
(Waits a while. She adjusts the light in the room)
(Telephone rings.)

Who's speaking?
I know your voice, but I don't know -

I know it very well. God I really think I must be going mad, No
your voice sounds just like, exactly like -

oh nonsense ... nonsense ...

what the time is? No idea ...

oh please ...
stop it ...

there's nothing I'd like better of course

Mother!
!!!!!

Please, I've had a whole evening of it. Mrs Borodon, it's *so* like
my mother's voice, please don't make fun of me.
Have mercy on me. Or let her say *something* which will make
me certain that it really is my mother.
Then I would go along with it.

Yes I remember that very well

yes I remember that too. Yes, we were together then, because Mia had gone with father to look at the horses. Yes, I remember it very clearly. I hardly dared to look in and you held me very tightly, you were frightened that I'd lose my balance and fall in.

Was *I* holding *you* tightly?
Really?
that's how you experienced it, the other way round?

you can't imagine that as a child, certainly not with your own mother. That you're holding *her* tightly, to stop her from -

what did you say?

Yes there was nobody else there, so I believe you, I believe you mother, my little mother. Come to me.
Say something else, say a little more.

What? Alone? But isn't it true that you meet all those other people again there?

No? But I thought -

But you weren't so alone here were you?

What about us?

And what about father then?

No I never realised that, I didn't know that.

But *mummy*, being alone isn't all that bad, they say that, if you just know how to love yourself -

no I'm not putting it right, I just mean: if you love yourself -

but why not?

No you weren't such a motherly mother but I didn't know any better then, you were just my mother. Our mother. I always used to hate it if you weren't at home. Doesn't that mean something to you?

What do you mean, inconsolable

So it stays the way it is at the moment and nothing is added and nothing is taken away?

So will you be feeling sick eternally, mother?
Oh dear -

But those kisses, that was really motherly

yes of course it came to an end

it's so amazing to hear your voice, so amazing, you can't imagine

so was that the only time in your life you were happy, because of
us?

Roll off which world?

That's nonsense. Well sorry.

What do you mean you didn't come to *give* us a goodnight kiss.

yes but nobody keeps a score of those things. Whether you give a
kiss or get a kiss, it amounts to the same thing, it doesn't - (matter)

and what if we just said: 'kissed each other' that's alright isn't it.

I don't know why you're going on about it, mother, they're only
words, and perhaps we'll never get this chance again and I so
wanted you to -

Look I really need -

I don't know, something more solid, something which will keep
me going for a while. I feel as though this is a very very very
distant long distance call and so you shouldn't just talk about the
weather.

What the weather *is* like?

Do you really want to know?

What did you say? Orgasm? Heavens! I've never heard you say
anything like that

No I can't suddenly do that, those kind of intimacies -

you weren't asking what? Whether I had them?

Oh, you weren't asking that. Then I misunderstood.
(Matter-of-factly) Yes, there's a lot written about that, there's a lot
of talk about that, that is indeed *the* great paradox, that the climax
of love is something that one experiences completely alone in one's
own body.
Why are you crying, don't cry mother.

My tone? What is wrong with my tone? I can't suddenly start
being 'sensitive'.
Don't cry, please, it's such a waste of time. Come on. Mother.
Please.
(Sits listening to the crying.)
Don't be so childish.
(Listens for a longer time.)
Oh go on then cry then.

No I don't mind

I don't mind.

Mrs Borodon, Mrs Borodon, she's crying the whole time, my
mother's crying like a -

Mother say something else, just say one more thing, please.
What did you say? I didn't catch it.

What? What? Tango? Town house? I can't make it out.

Fried potatoes?

Your shell collection?
(The phone has been hung up.)
The stub of a pencil?
(Silence)
(Dials number)
Robert, did I wake you up? I'm sorry, look this is the last time
I'll call you this evening, I'm really - (sorry)
Do you ever have that, a kind of feeling that you're getting bigger
and bigger, as big as the room, and in the meantime you carry on
talking and everything, but you do start wondering how you're
going to fit through the door? Or that you're getting very very

small, and you just carry on talking and everything, but you start wondering if the others can still see you, and you think it's odd that they don't seem to have noticed anything? Haven't you ever had that?

Never? I haven't either. I've never had that.

No, I've never had that, honest to god.
Go back to sleep, darling, sweet dreams.
(Hangs up. Telephone rings.)

Yes I was engaged. Have you found him?

Thank god.

Was he there?

And did you control yourself?

Yes I know - yes put him on.

Hello Nick, I expect you're furious with me.

Yes I know I promised, but we were worried.

You sometimes do things that I don't want you to do.
What? Weeing in girls' satchels for instance.

Well who does it then?

So it wasn't you that did it?
Why didn't you say so before?

You did say so?

On the way home?

What did your father do to you?

I can't make out what you're saying, you're shouting.

What?

Talked? He talked to you? And did you talk to him?

Why not? Full of *what*? I can't make out what - Oh, walnut whip.

Hello Mrs Gordon, thank goodness he turned up.
oh yes, I expect he was thirsty.

yes, goodbye Mrs Gordon, goodnight, don't mention it, goodnight.
(Dials)
Baz, it's me.
Me. From that prank about the chemists. Look I'm sorry I was so
stuffy about it.

I *have* got a sense of humour

but on Friday

not here. I've borrowed someone's else's house. But on *one*
condition. There'll be a man with me and I want you to get rid of
him. I've had enough of him. Do you understand?

No, you don't need to worry about that. He's just a spunkless
professor.

Will you do it?

No not now. I'll give you the address on Friday. Not today.

You can just say that you came to pick up the caracal.

The caracal.

Don't you know what that is? *(Laughs)*

I won't let on when you come in. He mustn't know that there's
anything between us. You rough him up so he leaves, and then...

Don't be so stupid, I'm not setting you up at all.

How can you know that?

What about me then, I'm taking a risk as well.

Well don't then. I thought I'd finally found a real man.
You're nothing but a bunch of pansies, the lot of you.

What I look like? Beautiful

yes

very beautiful. You won't be sorry. I'll pretend I'm not keen at first, then it won't look so suspicious.

Why would I do that, I'm not hard up. I'm a married woman, what would I need that for? I've got a lot more to lose than you! Okay?

Yes.

Your voice turns me on. So, the caracal.

Yes, the caracal. *(Hangs up.)*
(The telephone rings. She picks up the receiver and listens.)
Mia, I knew you were going to call.

What?

How I can do such a thing to you?

But if I just want to sit in my own living-room

Christ, if that's 'doing something to you'!

Oh is that so?

well if that's so

Mia stop screaming at me like that. I don't owe you a thing

Mia stop it, you'll be sorry later. Stop it, take a pill or something and calm down.

Okay. I'm a bloodless bitch in heat because I don't want that professor of yours in my bed

no that would really be the limit!

Jealous, Christ, of Simon? Of those spoilt brats of yours?

It's not a competition is it? It's all very simple with me. With you it's so much more fragile. And I will be going out New Year's Eve but that's the last time.
But you have to do *one* thing for me. Alex is coming to pick up the caracal, and I don't want to see him, so he's just dropping by to -

yes just to pick up the caracal.

yes he knows where it is. You've only got to answer the door.

It doesn't matter that you've never seen him

you just have to let him in

but it's better if he comes when I'm not there. That's not so terrible is it?

Well it's the least you can do for me.

Fine.

Fine.

Fine. *(Hangs up.)*
(Dials a number.)

I do apologise for calling so late, but could I just speak to your husband?

Oh, then I'll call back another time.

I'm from his office. I just went past the office actually, and I saw the light was still on, I thought that was a bit odd, so I thought I'd just call to be on the safe side

well no not directly from his office, from another office, but we do a lot of business and -

what did you say, closed down? I didn't know that, I hadn't heard that. That must have just happened then.

What did you say?

What did you say?

Is there something wrong?

No please I really don't mind

yes of course you mind terribly, but

What did you say? The business, sold?

He's living there now?

Where is it then?

Oh, in his old office, but where is that then

oh yes of course it's where it's always been and is he on the phone there?

The same number?

What's it listed under in the directory?

Under the name of the company? oh yes.

what hasn't he got any more?

A telephone?

No I, but it's already so late, I hope I didn't wake you up?

What do you mean, not at all any more? You must sleep during the day then?
I find that hard to believe. I think you do sleep, but that you don't notice you're doing it. Nobody could go that long without sleep. I recently heard about a drowning incident where someone had been in the water for three days and -

hello, hello, hello! *(The other end has rung off.)*
(Telephone rings.)

Sweetie, sweetie

no, that's not necessary Mia. It'll all be fine.
No you don't have to cancel it.
If you'll just stop crying. I *can't bear* it.
(Silence, she's thinking)
Hang on, there's someone at the door. I'll just go and answer it.
Hang on. *(Puts the receiver down on the table)*
(She walks round the table and picks the receiver up again.)
Darling, it's Alex. He's come to pick up the caracal, so you don't have to worry about that any more.

No I don't mind. It's just the way you're made.
I have to hang up. Tomorrow. *(Kiss, kiss)*

(Without hanging up, she immediately dials another number)

Yes, I'm just calling back because we got cut off and I thought
perhaps you thought I'd hung up

oh *you* hung up

oh I'm sorry, I didn't mean to -
but I didn't want to -

no you don't have to tell me

no-one else you can tell -

Because of another woman, but when did this -
But have you been this upset for a whole year?
And is he living there now with the other woman?

What do you mean, noble, perhaps she just couldn't cope with all
the fuss, perhaps she didn't dare to assume responsibility for
something so drastic, you don't know that, that doesn't mean that
she's noble.

Did he say that

Did he say that

did he say that

how long had he known her then?

But you can't know that, after three days.

What kind of position

that doesn't mean anything , there are so many people in that
type of social profession, that doesn't mean that in private they-

yes, in private, as a person, in daily life

what about you then?

Oh I don't know. But from what you've told me, I don't think
you need to be so terribly miserable

but you can't compare it to -

it's not a competition! No, really,

yes I understand, but I don't think it's really like that.
No I've got all the time in the world, it doesn't matter, perhaps
you'll feel better if you get it off your chest.

Yes.

Yes.

Yes. I don't know of course, but I have the feeling that he will
come back. Because what you were just saying about the other
woman, how he described her, people like that just don't exist.

No.

Yes.

no.

Goodnight. *(Hangs up. Looks at her watch.)*

(Dials number - the speaking clock - adjusts her watch.)

(Telephone rings. She doesn't answer it.)

Judith Herzberg

A writer who has built up an extensive body of work over thirty years
including poems, essays, plays, film scripts and television dramas with
many translations and adaptations to her name.

Her plays include:
1982 *Leedvermaak* for which she won the Critic's Prize and the
Charlotte Köhler Award.
1985 *En / Of*
1986 *Merg*, a libretto
1988 *Kras* for which she won the Dutch/Flemish Playwrights' Prize
1991 *Een goed hoofd*

A THREAD IN THE DARK

by Hella Haasse
translation by Della Couling

The play was awarded the Visser Neerlandia Prize in 1962 and has since been performed many times in Holland and Flanders.

In 1975 it was translated by Dick Hartoko and performed in the city of Jogjakarta, Java, Indonesia under the direction of Rendra, where the story was transposed to ancient Bali.

CHARACTERS

Minos, King of Crete
Ariadne, his eldest daughter
Phaedra, his youngest daughter
Nurse
High Priest
Theseus, son of the King of Athens
Skipper

SCENE 1

The palace of King Minos at Knossos on Crete. Ariadne's room.

ARIADNE *(caught in the oppression of a dream)* No! Don't go! Don't sail away without me! Don't leave me alone!

(Nurse and Phaedra enter. The Nurse is carrying clothes over her arm.)

PHAEDRA   Sister! Ariadne! What is it, what's the matter with you?

NURSE   She's dreaming. Wake her up. *(To herself)* Again the same, always the same; this is a bad omen.

PHAEDRA   Ariadne! Open your eyes.

ARIADNE *(Still half in the dream)* Don't leave me alone!

PHAEDRA   But I'm here. I'm with you. Wake up. You're dreaming, Ariadne.

ARIADNE   A dream? That dream was truer than reality. Oh Phaedra!

(She compulsively clings on to her sister.)

PHAEDRA   But what did you dream?

ARIADNE   I don't know any more. If only I knew.

NURSE   Don't ask. Don't talk about it.

ARIADNE   Was it ... like the other times? What did I say?

NURSE   Here's your tunic, your veil. Let me tie your sandals.

ARIADNE   Why won't you ever tell me afterwards what I said?

PHAEDRA   Does my sister often have such frightening dreams, Nurse? *(To Ariadne)* You've never told me that.

NURSE   Come here, your necklace, your bracelets.

ARIADNE   If you'd only tell me, then perhaps I could remember the dream.

NURSE   Hush now, don't think of it any more. Try never to recall dreams. The gods give you oblivion, consider yourself lucky. Doesn't life bring enough bitterness? Why should we suffer twice over through bad dreams?

ARIADNE   Yes, it *was* a bad dream. I can almost remember it. It was ...

NURSE   Talk of something else.

PHAEDRA   Hurry up, Ariadne, they're waiting for us. The ship from Athens has been in the harbour since sunrise. I saw the victims coming on to the quay.

NURSE   Seven beautiful girls, seven strapping young men.

PHAEDRA   Fairer and sturdier than us Cretans.

NURSE   Fourteen lives in their prime for our god in the labyrinth. Oh, he'll smile on us this year.

PHAEDRA   The son of the King of Athens is among them, as promised.

NURSE Did you see him?

PHAEDRA The victims went past under my window, on their way to the temple. He was walking in front of the others.

NURSE It'll be an impressive ceremony.

PHAEDRA Do you hear the crowd cheering outside? Hurry, Ariadne, they'll be arriving. *(At the window)* Yes, look, they've been consecrated, the victims, they're wearing white tunics and wreaths on their heads.

ARIADNE I don't want to see it.

NURSE *(pulls her to the window)* Oh, but do look. We've never had any like these before. We couldn't honour our god better.

ARIADNE Is that the son of the Athenian king?

PHAEDRA He's as handsome as a god himself.

ARIADNE What's his name?

PHAEDRA Theseus.

ARIADNE Oh, my dream!

NURSE Hush, child, that's over now.

ARIADNE I dreamt I was alone, doomed to die ...

PHAEDRA Yes? Tell us!

ARIADNE It's gone again.

PHAEDRA Come, they are waiting for us at the banquet.

ARIADNE I don't wish to celebrate, I can't.

NURSE It's a great day for Crete, the festival of the god under the ground.

ARIADNE They have to go into the labyrinth, as soon as the sun has set.

NURSE Of course, child. That is the custom. Let us be glad at the pleasure of our god tonight.

ARIADNE Horrible!

NURSE *(startled)* You don't know what you're saying.

ARIADNE But they'll be devoured. I can't bear that.

PHAEDRA Let us go now, Ariadne, or the celebrations will begin without us.

ARIADNE Where is the king?

NURSE In the throne room with the high priest.

ARIADNE Phaedra, stay here with Nurse.

PHAEDRA   You always want to do everything alone.

ARIADNE   I want to talk to my father.

NURSE   You may not disturb the king now. He's preparing himself for the sacrifice.

ARIADNE   This sacrifice is not going to take place.

NURSE   What did you say?

PHAEDRA   Why? Why won't it happen, Ariadne?

ARIADNE   I shall prevent it.

NURSE   Oh, oh! Mind your words, be careful!

ARIADNE   There shall be no more human sacrifices to the Minotaur.

NURSE   Hush! How dare you speak the name of our god so loudly. That is sacrilege. This is only allowed at the ceremony.

ARIADNE   He is not my god, the Minotaur.

NURSE   You're dreaming. You're still dreaming.

ARIADNE   No. Now I am wide awake. Now I know what I'm saying. I'm going to my father Minos.

NURSE *(to Phaedra)* Bring her to her senses.

PHAEDRA   They won't admit you to the king today. On the day of the ceremony he receives no-one, not even our mother, our brothers. You know that, Ariadne. Why do you want to speak to him?

ARIADNE   He must have the entrance to the labyrinth sealed up. Crete must forswear the Minotaur.

PHAEDRA   Oh, how dare you!

ARIADNE   Listen, must we let our lives be ruled by a monster who devours people?

NURSE   God under the ground, forgive her, she is a foolish child, blinded by pride ...

PHAEDRA   Ariadne, what are you thinking of? What are you trying to do?

ARIADNE   Put an end to the terror.

PHAEDRA   Sister, what is terrible about it?? This is a wonderful country. We are happy. We are rich. We are powerful. Nowhere in the world are people as fortunate as here. We have the finest houses, the most costly clothes. Nowhere is there such pomp and circumstance as here at the festivals in honour of our god ...

ARIADNE   Pomp and circumstance, yes. The whole city decorated, processions and carousing and dancing until sunrise, and every Cretan in their finest clothes, dripping gold and silver, drunk and delirious ... why? Because the Minotaur has been sated with human blood for yet another year!

PHAEDRA   Oh, you take everything so seriously.

NURSE   Enjoy life, my little dove.

ARIADNE   I can't enjoy a life bought with the death of others.

PHAEDRA   You've been at the festival year after year, from beginning to end ... You sang and danced with the rest of us, even after the victims had gone into the labyrinth. How could you do it then, Ariadne?

ARIADNE   Don't think I didn't care. I was full of fear and loathing, but I didn't know any better. I believed it had to be like that. I thought: the Minotaur is a severe god, his worship is the great tradition of our kingdom, our people. That is unalterable. Even I must bow to that. What mortal dares to question a god?

NURSE   That is so, my child, now you are talking sense. You are again what you should be, King Minos' eldest daughter, Ariadne, Princess of Crete.

ARIADNE   That's how I used to think.

NURSE   Yesterday, child. Yesterday you were still taking part in the preparations, here in the palace. And just now, when you woke up, you called for your ceremonial clothes and your jewels ...

ARIADNE   Is that so, Phaedra, is that really so?

PHAEDRA   What do I know about you? You have always said I was too young, too stupid, too frivolous. Yesterday I noticed nothing wrong with you. And this morning ... you had just had a bad dream, that's all.

ARIADNE   My dream!

NURSE   I know a wise woman, who can make a potion from herbs that helps against nightmares.

ARIADNE   But I don't want to forget.

NURSE Shall I call the king's interpreter of dreams? Perhaps he can give you comfort.

ARIADNE Flattery and deceit.

PHAEDRA What do you mean, he's amusing. He has an answer for everything. He even explains dreams to me that I invent, just for fun.

ARIADNE I want to remember *that* dream.

PHAEDRA Come on, have the interpreter of dreams come. Not today, but tomorrow, when the feasting is over, and our heads are too heavy from all the wine and dancing even to think.
(Her voice and gestures mimic an exaggeratedly servile court dignitary.)
Princess, to dream without knowing what, that is what we call the spring sickness of young maidens ...

ARIADNE Oh stop it, Phaedra.

NURSE Don't mock your sister.

PHAEDRA *(as before).* He will come from far over the sea, tall and slender and brave and blond as the sun. *(Suddenly she falls silent.)*

(Ariadne and Phaedra look at one another.)

Ah! Now I understand ... Ah, little sister!

(Ariadne turns away)

Poor Ariadne, you could never make a choice, and now you are making the wrong choice. A victim for our god!

ARIADNE *(sharply)* Be quiet!

PHAEDRA He is handsome, that's true. And strong. And still young. Isn't it a pity?

ARIADNE Shut up, Phaedra.

PHAEDRA When the ship landed, this morning, I thought: 'What a gift for the god!' Now that you desire him, I see he is a man ... and what a man, that Theseus.

ARIADNE Who told you I desire him?

PHAEDRA I saw your eyes when you looked at him.

ARIADNE   I curse the Minotaur, but not for Theseus' sake. I curse the Minotaur because he is evil without justice, without mercy. I'm going to my father.

PHAEDRA   But why are you in such a hurry suddenly? Just wait for one day, until after the festival. One sacrifice more or less, what difference does that make? You have a whole year to convince the king.

ARIADNE   Fourteen human lives are at stake.

PHAEDRA   Theseus is at stake.

ARIADNE   Crete is at stake.

PHAEDRA   Theseus!

ARIADNE   We are all at stake.

PHAEDRA   Theseus! Oh, I can understand it! But I don't have your courage, Ariadne. I would never dare defy a god as you are doing.

(Ariadne hurriedly leaves the room.)

NURSE   What have you done now with your talk! Instead of distracting her, you've made her cling stubbornly to that dangerous wickedness. Oh, nothing good can come of this. I've been afraid of it, ever since those dreams began.

PHAEDRA   But what does she dream?

NURSE   I don't know. I daren't think of it. She wrings her hands and screams ...

PHAEDRA   What does she scream? Come on, Nurse, come on, I shan't tell anyone about it. Tell your little Phaedra, then you've got it off your chest, that will do you good.

NURSE   Listen then, little dove ... She calls: don't leave me alone, don't you leave me alone! She screams names ...

PHAEDRA   What names? Tell me, Nurse, tell me!

NURSE   Phaedra! Theseus!

PHAEDRA   Theseus! Phaedra!?

NURSE   Hush! Be quiet! What have I said?

SCENE 2

Throne room in the palace.

HIGH PRIEST They refuse the poppy drink. They say they want no
　　drugs.
MINOS 　　　Aren't they afraid, then?
HIGH PRIEST Apparently not, Sire. In them I have seen neither
　　fear nor ecstasy, as in the victims of former years.
MINOS 　　　That will probably change towards evening. The day
　　is still young. They are strangers here, they don't know our
　　customs. They know nothing of our god. I wonder if they even
　　have any idea of him. Well, I shall come and look at them myself
　　directly.
HIGH PRIEST One of them asks to talk to you, Sire.
MINOS 　　　That has never happened before.
HIGH PRIEST It's the son of the King of Athens.
MINOS 　　　He's consecrated to the god, he does not have a name
　　any more, he is no-one.
HIGH PRIEST He says he must speak with you about an important
　　matter for Crete.
MINOS 　　　On behalf of his father?
HIGH PRIEST He did not want to take me into his confidence.
MINOS 　　　He is not an ambassador, but a sacrifice. I have
　　nothing to discuss with him. Someone is at the door. See who it is.
HIGH PRIEST It's the princess, your daughter Ariadne.
MINOS *(to Ariadne)* Who let you in here, while I'm speaking in
　　private with the high priest?
ARIADNE 　　The guard did his duty, he wanted to prevent me.
MINOS 　　　You have never disobeyed me before.
ARIADNE 　　This is not a day like other days.
MINOS 　　　For that very reason I demand even greater obedience.
ARIADNE 　　On the day of the sacrifice the king receives supp-
　　licants. That is the law here on Crete. I have a request for you.
MINOS 　　　You know the law better than I, it appears.

HIGH PRIEST She is right, Sire. No Cretan has ever made use of the privilege. We on this island have everything our hearts desire. But the law exists, it's true.

MINOS Because you have such a good memory, daughter ... you may ask.

ARIADNE Then listen to him, the one who has requested an interview with you.

MINOS Since when have you become an advocate of the victims?

ARIADNE I heard what was said here, when I came in.

MINOS Those are my affairs.

ARIADNE He is the son of a king.

MINOS I can afford to deny kings I have conquered in war. The Athenians are my slaves. They send me tributes, and sacrifices for our god. That is my right.

ARIADNE They must die in the labyrinth.

MINOS That is an honour for them.

ARIADNE I plead the law.

MINOS That is not valid for victims. They are outside the law.

ARIADNE I implore you: let the son of the King of Athens have his say.

MINOS *(to High Priest)* Bring him here.

(High Priest leaves.)

I don't understand what has possessed you. You should be sitting at the banquet. What my sons would not dare, you have dared to do.

ARIADNE Father, do away with the sacrifices.

MINOS Do away with the ...?

(He stares at her, then starts laughing, but without kindness.)
My daughter, you have gone mad. What is our god supposed to feed on, if I do away with the sacrifices?

ARIADNE Let him starve.

MINOS   *(Half rises from his throne).* Anyone else would pay
with his life for those words.

ARIADNE   That is why I say them.

(The High Priest enters with Theseus)

HIGH PRIEST Here he is, the one I spoke of, Sire.

THESEUS   My name is Theseus.

MINOS   Here you are not a person, but consecrated sacrificial
flesh.

THESEUS   This flesh still has a heart and brain and a voice.

MINOS   Make use of them as long as you still can; that's a
short time.

THESEUS   Let me go first into the cave ... alone, before the
others.

MINOS   Even as a group you'll all be alone in there in the
dark, each for himself ... But good, granted.

THESEUS   I want my sword back, that was taken from me.

HIGH PRIEST Definitely not! Impossible! Sacrilege!

THESEUS   Then does your god not offer combat?

HIGH PRIEST It would be pointless. Our god is invincible.

THESEUS   I'm not going to meet death without my sword.

MINOS   Do so then, my good fellow, do so.

HIGH PRIEST But Sire, it's against the rules. Victims have
always been unarmed.

MINOS *(annoyed)* Let us make an exception here. What does it
matter?

HIGH PRIEST It will create a precedent.

MINOS   Why? He's a special case. A king's son. His father
has no other sons. We shall never get any more princes from
Athens. And furthermore, I repeat: what does it matter? Give
him his sword.

THESEUS   I wish to add that I intend to fight your god.

HIGH PRIEST Outrageous, Sire, that attitude cannot be allowed.

MINOS *(yawns)* Let him. *(Softly to the High Priest)* Consider:
what difference does it make?

THESEUS   I do not believe in the invincibility of your god.

MINOS   No? Before we are twenty-four hours older, you will believe in him, be sure of that. But now something else. You had something important to tell me relating to Crete. I haven't heard that yet.

THESEUS   The death of the god that protects you means the end of Crete's power.

HIGH PRIEST That kind of thing gets known, Sire. Such words spread like wildfire. They penetrate where they can do damage, like poison, like a disease.

MINOS   Lock him in a dungeon until this evening. Then he can't brag at the feast, when everyone is present. No-one has yet heard what he said except us here. At sunset he'll enter the labyrinth. He'll never come back.

HIGH PRIEST But his companions think as he does.

MINOS   Then throw them all in the dungeon. Place him in isolation. Away with him. Call the guard.

ARIADNE *(to High Priest)* Don't forget to give him his sword. The king has promised.

THESEUS *(only now really noticing Ariadne)* My thanks ... Lady.

(Guards surround Theseus. Led by the High Priest they lead him away.)

ARIADNE   Spare Theseus. Send him back to Athens with his friends.

MINOS   Why should I do that?

ARIADNE   The sacrificing of people is unworthy. A stain on your name, on the name of Crete.

MINOS   You speak like a rebel. Who has put these words into your head?

ARIADNE   My reason, my heart.

MINOS   And you are Minos' daughter, my own flesh and blood. I always loved you most of my children, I let you dance on my knee.

ARIADNE   I haven't changed, father.

MINOS   You've never given me trouble. You've never made foolish demands, you've never wanted the moon out of the heavens.

ARIADNE   So let me just once have my way. Do away with the sacrifices.

MINOS   I wonder if you are not particularly stupid ... or particularly dangerous.

ARIADNE   I am trying to be honest and open.

MINOS   It would seriously worry me if I felt you were speaking the truth. But you are not. You have the good taste to lie.

ARIADNE   No, I am not lying.

MINOS   Don't say the same thing twice, that betrays little power of invention. You are lying, because it's not true you are trying to be honest. How could you be? It's to do with him, who was here just now. You want to help him. But is that necessary? He seems quite determined to help himself. He's going to challenge the god.

ARIADNE   But that is certain death.

MINOS   Don't say that. He has a chance. Everyone who goes into the labyrinth has a chance, after all.

ARIADNE   That is sophistry. You want to soothe me with that, just as perhaps, year in year out, you give the victims hope. False hope, for no-one has ever come back. No-one can ever come back. The Minotaur devours all the victims, every last one of them. Do away with the sacrifice, father!

(High Priest, who has come in while Ariadne is speaking, stops, terrified.)

MINOS *(to High Priest)* You hear that. What do you say to it?

HIGH PRIEST Sire, I am speechless.

MINOS   The whole world trembles before our god. On Crete no-one dares to speak his name aloud. But my daughter here wants to do away with him!

(To Ariadne) Listen, don't you understand that Crete owes its glory and wealth and power to the existence of the Minotaur in the labyrinth? Abroad, our success is attributed to the aid and protection of our god. Look at the Cretans, they say, what perseverance, what courage. Their god gives them strength! What a god that must be! Compared with him, those gods of ours are but urchins! ... Do you understand me, daughter? Wherever you go, to the islands, to Egypt, or to the mainland in the north, everywhere they are openly or secretly afraid of the Minotaur, of Crete, of me. That is why we are invincible. Whoever knows how to handle fear as a weapon, rules the world.

ARIADNE A god who wishes to be served by fear, cannot be a true god.

HIGH PRIEST Princess, be careful now. There are things one may not think, let alone speak aloud.

ARIADNE Chase him back into the underworld, where he came from.

HIGH PRIEST Sire, she is sick, she is raving.

MINOS Come, I shall make my wise daughter even wiser. Ariadne, the Minotaur is not a god.

HIGH PRIEST Sire ...!

ARIADNE A monster, then, that no-one dare oppose! That's what I've always thought. A monster.

MINOS There is no Minotaur at all, daughter.

HIGH PRIEST *(trembling, alarmed)* You yourself said it, Sire.

MINOS Yes, yes, yes. And so what? At the time I said: there is a Minotaur ... and lo, there *was* a Minotaur. And I alone have the right to say: the Minotaur does not exist. Whenever I want, and to whom I want, and that is that.

ARIADNE The Minotaur doesn't exist ...?

MINOS That is so. An invention of mine, this Minotaur. A brilliant idea. Pity there are only three people to appreciate it: I, the High Priest here, and you. What do you say to it?

ARIADNE Why did you do it?

MINOS For power, my daughter, for power. Just think: without needless use of force I bend Crete to my will, with the aid of Cretans I can rule over land and sea - and all that through a name, an idea, a spectre: the Minotaur.

ARIADNE   And human sacrifices are made to this shadow?

MINOS   Thanks to those sacrifices the Minotaur becomes reality for friend and foe.

ARIADNE   But where do the victims go, what happens to them?

MINOS   They perish through their own fear. You forget the labyrinth, that great work of the late Daedalos, my architect.

ARIADNE   You had the labyrinth built with the intention of ...

MINOS   Ah, what intelligence you have. You understand half a word. What good would the Minotaur have been to me without that underground network of passages no-one ever enters of his own free will?

ARIADNE   It's horrible ...

MINOS   Anyone who doesn't know the ground plan will never, never find the way out of the labyrinth. I have destroyed Daedalos' drawings. A precautionary measure, should someone be able to return to say that the Minotaur does not exist. But no-one ever comes back. If they don't starve to death down there in the darkness, they commit suicide by strangling themselves with their belts.

ARIADNE   I demand from you the life of Theseus of Athens and his companions.

MINOS   You demand? On what grounds?

ARIADNE   On the grounds of your deceit.

MINOS   My interests, Crete's interests, are yours.

ARIADNE   Never, I shall go out into the streets, through the town, through the market, along the harbour, I shall knock on every door, throw open the windows and shout it out: the Minotaur does not exist!

MINOS   They would seize you and take you bound to the madhouse ... if they didn't stone you to death on the spot for naming the name of their god.

ARIADNE   There are perhaps some who would believe me, for whom my words would mean salvation. They will help me.

MINOS You are mistaken. If there were such, they would keep silent to save their own skins.

ARIADNE Are Cretans such cowards?

MINOS They love their lives.

ARIADNE You have made them so afraid?

MINOS I? Not I, daughter. They have made themselves afraid. They have given my idea, the Minotaur, shape and inflated it with their own imagination. He stamps and snorts and roars and spreads death and destruction, driven by what lives in every Cretan of secret hatred and resentment and black thoughts and suppressed appetites. That fear is holy, because it's their very own fear, although they don't realise it. They are ready to stifle that fear with human sacrifice.

ARIADNE Spare the Athenians!

MINOS I dare not. My people demand the ceremony. They won't be deprived of the annual propitiation of the god.

ARIADNE I shall give gold, jewels, precious objects to buy sacrificial animals for it, they could drive whole herds into the labyrinth.

MINOS They want people for the god.

ARIADNE You uphold the sacrifices, not they. You have an interest in their fear.

MINOS Who am I? It is the power of Crete that's at stake. That is of interest for all Cretans

ARIADNE Oh, a labyrinth of cunning and lies.

MINOS The labyrinth is the national symbol.

(Ariadne buries her face in her hands.)

Prove your intelligence. Accept things as they are.

HIGH PRIEST Sire, are you not afraid she will speak?

MINOS She realises very well it's useless. Ariadne, nothing prevents me from offering my own daughter to the god.

ARIADNE I know that.

MINOS *(pensively)* It would be a new, unprecedented triumph for the Minotaur.

ARIADNE Of course.

MINOS   What a bond, almost of kinship, between me and him. The people would honour me as a demi-god. If I so wished, Cretans would go to the ends of the earth for me. They would fetch me the sun from the heavens. There is no country I could not conquer in this way, no people I could not enslave.

ARIADNE   Yes.

MINOS   In spite of yourself you would be my instrument, and help to consolidate my power. Your name would be coupled with that of the Minotaur for evermore. So be reasonable and don't force me to do what ...

(Ariadne quickly leaves the room.)

HIGH PRIEST Sire, I am uneasy. There lives no woman in the world who can keep a secret.

MINOS   What an idea that was of mine, what a brilliant notion. Minos gives the Minotaur his own daughter ...

HIGH PRIEST   But Sire, you would not ...?

MINOS   Sacrifice her? We shall give it a different name. I am thinking of a marriage. Ah, just think about it: Crete celebrates the wedding of Minos' daughter Ariadne with the Minotaur. King Minos, the father-in-law of a god. What a celebration, what an extraordinary ceremony. We must think about it in detail. This knife cuts both ways: more glory for Crete, as well as an elegant way of preventing my daughter Ariadne speaking out of turn.

HIGH PRIEST   Your own child, Sire ...

MINOS   And? What do my power and success mean to her? Nothing. What follows? That she doesn't feel as a daughter should. And if she doesn't, then she's not my daughter. And if she's not my daughter, then I can regard her as a danger. What prevents me from removing a danger? Heh? And what prevents me sending you with her as her major-domo, if you no longer like it here in my service?

HIGH PRIEST A misunderstanding, Sire. I never for one moment maintained that your idea was not a stroke of genius.

MINOS   Then make all the arrangements. Make it credible, spare neither expense nor effort. That's your job, that's why I made you high priest.

HIGH PRIEST *(hastily)* I see it all before me: the procession, the ceremony at the entrance to the labyrinth, the bride bedecked with flowers going to meet the god, a choir singing anthems ...

MINOS *(leans back comfortably)* We invite foreign guests. Huge crowds will come flocking. Grandstands, triumphal arches, huge outlay. At least a week of festivities, including banquets and bull games.

HIGH PRIEST   I shall draw up a plan, Sire.

MINOS   Immediately after the sacrificial ceremony is over, the news of the wedding can be announced. I shall keep my daughter in isolation. Let it be known she is preparing in silence for the great event, then it won't cause surprise if she is not seen about any more.

HIGH PRIEST   As you wish, Sire.

MINOS   That's that. And now to business. Today ...

SCENE 3

Ariadne's room. Enter Phaedra and Nurse

PHAEDRA   If she stays away any longer, we shall arrive too late at the banquet. And I don't want to miss the bull games.

NURSE   Let's hope for the best. How could my little dove, my golden heart, forget herself in such a way?

PHAEDRA   Oh, it's time she married and had children.

NURSE   Quiet, I think I hear her footsteps in the gallery.

ARIADNE *(enters, out of breath)* Phaedra!
(She throws her arms round her sister.)

PHAEDRA   The king must have been furious with you.

NURSE *(kneels beside Ariadne, busies herself with her clothes)* Oh, I was really frightened. You should have listened to me. Look, your clothes are all a mess from running so fast, you've torn your veil.

ARIADNE   Phaedra! Phaedra!

PHAEDRA   What's happened?

ARIADNE   Phaedra, the Minotaur does not exist!

PHAEDRA   Who says so?

ARIADNE   The king himself.

PHAEDRA   That can't be true.

ARIADNE   Look at me. There is no Minotaur. There has never been a Minotaur. Listen: the Minotaur is an invention of King Minos. A fairy tale to make people afraid!

NURSE   Oh hush, my little heart, my child. You're feverish. Let me put you to bed and look after you.

ARIADNE   People are sacrificed to this non-existent Minotaur. Year in, year out, all Crete takes part in a pointless, bloody charade.

PHAEDRA   So no-one is devoured, then. Is that so terrible?

ARIADNE   A monster in the labyrinth ... that was bad, but it was a real danger, that we could have fought, that we could have freed ourselves from. No monster in the labyrinth is infinitely worse ... for think, Phaedra, where lurks the danger now? In Cretans themselves, and in the power that makes them dance to its tune, in Minos ...

NURSE   Do not judge, the king is your father!

PHAEDRA   I would think you'd be relieved, now you know the Minotaur doesn't exist.

ARIADNE   Only since I've known it do I realise what fear and horror are.

NURSE   Here, let me take off that tight headband for you ...

ARIADNE   Leave me alone. I'm not sick. Phaedra, do you realise what the Minotaur is?

PHAEDRA *(airily)* If he's not real, he is at any rate a clever invention.

ARIADNE *(stares at her astonished)* I shall have no peace until everyone knows.

NURSE   Oh child, be careful. Don't talk about it, forget it even.

ARIADNE   But it's the truth.

NURSE *(raises her hands)* Who dares say what truth is and what is not?

ARIADNE I'm repeating the words of King Minos. The Minotaur does not exist. You do believe me?

NURSE *(evasively)* Sometimes it's better to avoid the truth.

ARIADNE Why?

NURSE I've lived longer than you, I know the world, people. This I know: whoever pursues truth can expect misfortune.

ARIADNE I'm not afraid.

NURSE But I'm afraid, I'm afraid for you, my little dove. You only have one life. Don't go looking for trouble. Be sensible. Be a good, wise child. Listen: you dreamed it. You haven't been with the king. You've been lying here asleep.

ARIADNE *(pulls herself free)* No!

NURSE You dreamed it! *(kneeling)* God in the labyrinth, she's out of her mind, don't be angry; I shall burn incense, day and night, and offer libations of wine and say the prayers that she withholds from you ...

ARIADNE Stop it, there's no god down there. There's nothing to be afraid of.

NURSE Ruler under the earth, I'm not listening to her. I don't believe her! I believe in you, hail to you, hail to you ...

ARIADNE But you, Phaedra. You don't believe in that spectre. Tell me you don't believe in it?

PHAEDRA *(shrugs)* What happens now with Theseus?

ARIADNE I must save him.

PHAEDRA Of course. It would be a thousand pities to sacrifice him to ... nothing.

ARIADNE The labyrinth is constructed in such a way that even with a light no-one can ever find the way back.

PHAEDRA Isn't there a map?

ARIADNE Minos has destroyed it.

PHAEDRA What will you do then ...?

ARIADNE *(suddenly)* Nurse!

NURSE Yes, child.

ARIADNE   Get me a ball of thin, strong thread. A big ball of
very fine thread, but strong as iron.

(Nurse leaves the room shaking her head.)

PHAEDRA   You mean ... a long thread, an unbreakable thread for
Theseus?

ARIADNE   A thread in the dark of the labyrinth.

PHAEDRA   Why is it always you who can think up such things?

ARIADNE   Listen, you can help me, you know. You must go
with me when I take the ball to Theseus.

PHAEDRA   At the banquet? Under the eyes of father and the
court and all Crete?

ARIADNE   Theseus is sitting in the deepest cave in the dungeons
under the palace, because he said he wanted to challenge the
Minotaur.

PHAEDRA   And the Minotaur doesn't exist!

ARIADNE   Theseus doesn't know that! I must be the one to tell
him. I can give him two certainties before he goes into the
labyrinth this evening: the thread, that is freedom. And this: the
Minotaur doesn't exist, that is life!

PHAEDRA   How will you get into the prison? How are we to slip
past the guards? You know it's impossible.

ARIADNE   Every year you give a trinket to the victims, a
personal gift from you for the Minotaur.

PHAEDRA   That's what father wants. The daughters of the king
should honour the god. Because I'm so obedient it's less
noticeable that you don't do it any more.

ARIADNE   As the victims won't be sitting at the banquet today,
you can't hand over the votive offering for the god personally.
Isn't it obvious that you go down to the dungeon, to him, the most
important offering, Theseus of Athens? You stay with the guard,
far from the stinking cave, and you send your maid to the
prisoner...

PHAEDRA   My maid?

ARIADNE Me, in disguise. I don't need much time. Oh, from now on I desire nothing more than readiness of speech, powers of persuasion ...

PHAEDRA If Theseus comes back from the labyrinth ... what then?

ARIADNE He must appear, when the sun is rising, early tomorrow morning, and show himself to the people gathered drinking and dancing in front of the entrance to the cave. He must shout: I am free! You are all free! The Minotaur does not exist!

PHAEDRA They wouldn't believe him.

ARIADNE Yes they would. They'll believe him because he's come back. No-one has ever come back before.

PHAEDRA Yes, but ...

ARIADNE What deeds of the king, what words of the high priest, can give Theseus the lie! To prove they were in the right they would have to show the Minotaur living or dead to the people ... and they can't do that, they can never, never do that. They'll be forced to admit openly there is no Minotaur!

PHAEDRA And then?

ARIADNE The Cretans will have become wiser. They'll reject a rule that's based on lies. Theseus will return unharmed to Athens.

PHAEDRA And you? And I?

ARIADNE Don't be afraid, Phaedra. Realise what this means: to destroy the terror of the Minotaur. To free Crete, the whole world, of fear.

PHAEDRA But perhaps the people don't want to be free of the Minotaur. How do you know they'll be thankful for the news that he doesn't exist?

ARIADNE Who can want his own fear?

PHAEDRA Not my own fear, but the fear of others.

ARIADNE Phaedra, you can't really mean what you are saying. Not you, little sister.

PHAEDRA Little children grow up.

ARIADNE Will you help me?

PHAEDRA Yes, on one condition.

ARIADNE What is it?

PHAEDRA   If it's ever discovered, then say I acted in good faith. Say I knew nothing about it.

ARIADNE   I take full responsibility. Quiet, here comes Nurse with the thread.

SCENE 4

Ariadne's room, later. Ariadne is walking restlessly up and down.

ARIADNE   I couldn't tell him what he has to do before he leaves Crete. And that's the main thing, Phaedra, that's what I should have done. I want him to appear in front of everyone, unscathed, and call out: the Minotaur does not exist!

PHAEDRA   He wants to take you with him to Athens, he wants to marry you. He promised you that?

ARIADNE   Tonight, when everyone is dancing and celebrating, I'll try to slip into the cave again. I'll keep watch at the place where Theseus has fastened the end of the thread. Then I shall catch him as soon as he comes back ...

PHAEDRA   He said you must go to the ship. Do you still know the password? Aethra, the name of his mother.

ARIADNE   I'm not leaving before I've destroyed the Minotaur in the minds of the Cretans.

PHAEDRA   Imagine, he has scarcely seen you and he wants to make you his wife. Now you must be beside yourself with joy. You do love him, Ariadne?

ARIADNE   I don't know. As soon as I saw him in the sacrificial procession, under our window this morning, I knew I had to meet him, him alone. I can't remember my dream, but he was part of it. Perhaps it is preordained that with him, by him, the lie of the Minotaur is destroyed.

PHAEDRA   I'm afraid, Ariadne.

ARIADNE   I've promised you nothing will happen to you. I'll keep my word.

PHAEDRA   Let's run away. Let's make sure we're safe, before the king notices anything.

ARIADNE   You go to the ship, you know the password.

PHAEDRA   Alone?

ARIADNE   Whatever happens to me, you'll be safe on board.
For my sake Theseus will want to take you with him.

PHAEDRA   For your sake, always for your sake. Why not for
mine?

(Nurse enters)

NURSE   Ariadne! King Minos has ordered you have to keep
to your room.

ARIADNE   For how long?

NURSE   I don't know, I heard it from the chief of the palace
guard.

PHAEDRA   Do you hear that, Ariadne, we're being watched.

ARIADNE   I'm being watched, not you.

(The sound of horns is heard outside)

NURSE   The sun is setting. The ceremony's beginning. If you go
and stand at the window, you'll still be able to see the victims
being taken away. From the gates of the palace to the entrance to
the cave, a huge sea of people. There are more soldiers there than
in other years, forming a cordon.

ARIADNE *(suddenly, decisively)* Nurse, lend me your cloak and
shawl. Don't ask me any questions, I can tell you nothing. Only
this: neither Phaedra nor I will ever come back here. Dear Nurse
... hide far away from here, in some village in the hills, where no
one knows that you brought up King Minos' daughters.

NURSE *(bewildered)* But child ... my children ...

ARIADNE *(to Phaedra)* Come. I'll take you to the ship. Then I'm
going back to the cave.

ACT TWO

SCENE 1

*Theseus' ship. Night time. Ariadne, in conversation with the
Skipper, is walking up and down the deck. Phaedra has made
herself comfortable on a coil of rope.*

SKIPPER   I can do nothing about it, I obey the orders my master
gave me before he went on land. Set sail after sunset, as in the
agreement with King Minos of Crete ... and then later, after
nightfall, come back secretly and drop anchor in this bay. If my
master and his companions don't give the signal in the course of
the night here on the coast, I must leave for Athens before sunrise.

ARIADNE   But I want to go on land.

SKIPPER   But I can't sail inshore now.

ARIADNE   You raised the anchor without warning me.

SKIPPER   You came with the password 'Aethra'. I thought you
would stay on board.

ARIADNE   Set me down on land somewhere. Here, all the jewels
I have on me are yours.

SKIPPER   If you offered me a thousand times as much, I
couldn't go closer inshore. I have my orders.

ARIADNE   I am the daughter of King Minos.

SKIPPER   I am the grand-nephew of Zeus Almighty.

ARIADNE   Good, then I'll swim to land.

SKIPPER   You can save yourself the trouble. I see torches on
the shore. The agreed sign. That means my master's now waiting
on the beach.

ARIADNE   I have no gods to pray to, but you, Athenian, thank
Zeus and whatever else their names are, that Theseus has come
back from the labyrinth.

SKIPPER   I have always had faith in my master's sword.

ARIADNE   He can't have gone far, nor have descended very
deep. So he did believe me. He has really come back.

PHAEDRA   Look, the light of the torches is moving up and down.

SKIPPER *(to the sailors)* Hoist the sails! Make for the shore!

PHAEDRA Ariadne! Theseus has come back alive from the labyrinth.

ARIADNE If only I'd been able to wait for him at the entrance ...

PHAEDRA Listen, in the distance you can hear the music and the shouts of the people at the festival ground in front of the cave. You know yourself what goes on there after midnight. Who could guarantee they would have been sober enough to understand Theseus' message? Perhaps they would have trampled you both down in their drunken state.

ARIADNE But we should be there now, not here.

PHAEDRA Why aren't you glad we are safe? No-one saw Theseus and his friends escape, no-one knows we have fled. Before it's light we shall be out at sea, beyond the reach of father's ships.

ARIADNE I must run for cover with a truth that concerns everyone on Crete? I'm not a thief.

PHAEDRA Why are you so determined to bring us into danger?

ARIADNE Theseus will not want to sail away without doing what I ask of him.

PHAEDRA How do you know that?

ARIADNE He came to Crete to kill the Minotaur, to free the world from a monster. He's found here more than a monster of flesh and blood. This is a difficult task, rightly a task for a hero. He'll not want to go away before he has accomplished that.

PHAEDRA You have scarcely spoken ten words to him. Do you know him so well now?

ARIADNE He fights monsters and giants to help the defenceless and enslaved, to deliver the world from fear and misery.

SKIPPER *(to the sailors)* Watch out, watch out for rocks, underwater reefs! Oars up, hold! Drop the anchor, we're in shallow water. *(Calls to the shore)* Theseus! Master! You must wade through the surf, we can't come any closer to the shore!

PHAEDRA They're putting out the torches, they're entering the water! Ariadne, just think; in one single day our whole life has changed. Last night I lay wide awake thinking of the sacrificial

feast, and now I'm here with you on the way to a distant country.
Look, Theseus is climbing on board!

THESEUS   I have killed the Minotaur!

(The crew cheer)

ARIADNE   Theseus ...

SKIPPER   These two women came on board with the password.

THESEUS   Welcome aboard my ship, Ariadne. The Minotaur is
dead.

SKIPPER *(to the sailors)* Raise the anchor! Shift the helm! We are
making for the open sea! To Athens, boys, home!

ARIADNE   Theseus!

THESEUS *(to his companions)* See here the princess of Crete, King
Minos' daughter, who helped me to escape from the labyrinth,
after I had killed the monster.

SKIPPER   Put on full sail, the morning wind is coming to our
aid!

ARIADNE   Theseus, tell the skipper he must lower the anchor
again. We cannot leave yet!

THESEUS   Don't be afraid of the unknown. It's a good ship, the
season is favourable. In Athens the people will worship you out of
gratitude for your part in my return home. My old father will
welcome you as though you were his own daughter.

ARIADNE   But listen to me ...

SKIPPER   Master, down there on the deck are the sailors, they
want to hear how you killed the monster. Speak to them, Master,
give an account of your fight!

THESEUS *(goes to the edge of the upper deck)* In short then, men,
more later. I crept along, groping along the walls of the passage-
way, I sought my way. The stink of rotting flesh assailed me from
invisible pits and holes. A god must have led my footsteps.
Somewhere in the depths I heard a muffled roar that almost froze
the blood in my veins ... Echoes rolled ominously through that
network of underground tunnels, like a far distant storm. If I had
not borne constantly in mind that my life and those of my fellow

victims depended on the outcome of the fight, I would have gone
back. I have defied many dangers in my life, but I have never gone
through anything that can be compared with the adventure in that
cave. Words fail me, now that I must recount it. I knew that you,
my companions, were waiting up there in that entrance, black as
the jaws of the underworld, in fearful suspense. I did not want to
betray your trust. I gripped more firmly the hilt of my sword. I
felt the thread on my belt. Step by step I descended into that black
darkness. I sensed that something was coming towards me out of
the caverns and holes down there, I heard the dragging sound of a
heavy body, the scraping of claws over the stones, and a panting, a
fierce snarl. Suddenly a faint, greenish light. Around me I saw a
cave of gigantic dimensions, and in that room I stood finally face
to face with the Minotaur ...

ARIADNE   No!

THESEUS   You need not be afraid. It's all over now. The
monster is dead, I am here, unharmed.

ARIADNE   Give the skipper the order to turn back, to land, go
among the Cretans who are celebrating the sacrifice and shout out
there, as loudly as you can, what you have told here. Go to the
room where my father is gathered with the high priest and all the
nobles and shout in their faces: I have killed the Minotaur! Run
through the streets, shake the people awake from their drunken
torpor and shout at them: the Minotaur is dead!

THESEUS   That is pointless. I have fulfilled my task by felling
the monster. I am not going to risk my life to no purpose. The
Cretans will learn soon enough that the Minotaur doesn't exist
any more.

ARIADNE   Do it, for my sake. I desire no other thanks for the
thread I brought you.

THESEUS   I will take you with me to Athens, I have promised
you marriage. Is that not a princely thanks?

ARIADNE   But I ask for nothing but this one thing: that you
confide your heroic act to Crete, that you tell Crete that the
Minotaur does not exist.

THESEUS   That is true, the Minotaur exists no longer. He's lying in that cave there deep under the ground, in a pool of black blood, a gigantic mass of decomposing flesh.

ARIADNE   There has never been a Minotaur. Never! Never! The labyrinth is empty.

THESEUS   Who claims that?

ARIADNE   My father, King Minos. The Minotaur is his invention: a spectre to frighten the world with. I still hear his words ringing in my ears: The Minotaur does not exist!

THESEUS   He told you a lie.

ARIADNE   If the Minotaur really existed, my father would not have dared to mock a god that has made Crete mighty.

THESEUS   Believe me, there was a Minotaur in the labyrinth, and one that exceeded my wildest expectations.

ARIADNE   Have them turn the helm, lower the anchor, take me with you to the shore, into the labyrinth, and show me the body of the Minotaur.

THESEUS   You are mad. I killed the monster, now that's enough. There's nothing left for me to do here, I want to go back to Athens.

ARIADNE   But I demand it.

THESEUS   You must take my word for it. The Minotaur is dead.

ARIADNE   There has never been a living Minotaur.

THESEUS   I don't want to lose patience. You have placed yourself under my protection. You are my bride. Go to sleep, Ariadne. In the morning, when you see the sun shining on the blue sea, you will have forgotten the Minotaur.

ARIADNE   Never.

THESEUS   You won't have any more doubts.

(Ariadne turns away.)

And you, little one, with the lively eyes, who are you?

PHAEDRA   Phaedra, King Minos' youngest daughter.

SCENE 2

Early the next morning. Theseus is asleep on deck. Ariadne comes slowly up to him, she stands looking at him, and replaces an end of his cloak which had fallen off, over him. He wakes up.

THESEUS   Ariadne?

ARIADNE   The wind is cool. Sleep on.

THESEUS   No, stay. You are awake early.

ARIADNE   I haven't slept.

THESEUS   That little sister of yours, did she lie awake too?

ARIADNE   Phaedra is sleeping. As soon as she has closed her eyes, she has let go of reality and breathes deeply and calmly ... like all children.

THESEUS   Although I'm not a child any more, I too slept dreamlessly. But who could wonder at that, after yesterday.
(Ariadne suddenly turns away.)
I didn't suffer any wounds, it's true - which in itself might be called a wonder - but I was exhausted.
(Ariadne does not move.)
It's behind us. I have done what I had to do, what was expected of me. I can meet my father and my people with a light heart.
(Ariadne does not move.)
Ariadne, the greatest task lies before me. My father is old, he won't live much longer. Athens, that has sustained so many blows, that has been ravaged by war, where trade has been halted ... I must restore my Athens to its former glory. Look, what they need there more than anything else is a strong man, a true ruler, a leader-king, whom they can respect, whom they will follow through thick and thin. I want to be that leader.
(Ariadne does not move.)
And I shall be that leader. Perhaps I've been lucky. Fate has always given me the chance to do something. I've never had to resort to fine words and promises. I've always been able to act. What is more convincing than actions? My father's subjects have a rockhard faith in me - I cannot disappoint that. Believe me, the

Athenians are counting on my return. If you knew how that gave me strength yesterday in the labyrinth: the realisation that over there in my native city they knew I would slay the Minotaur.

ARIADNE   But you didn't slay the Minotaur!

THESEUS   Why won't you grant me the Minotaur, Ariadne?

ARIADNE   Prove to me that you killed him. You can't. You have no wound, no dent in your sword, no blood on your clothes. Neither hide nor hair of the Minotaur. What will you show to the Athenians as evidence of your heroic deed?

THESEUS   My return. They won't ask for more.

ARIADNE   I ask for more.

THESEUS   But I have helped you. I have freed your people, I killed the Minotaur.

ARIADNE   You had the chance to rid Crete of a peril a thousand times more terrible than a monster of flesh and blood ... the fear of something that does not exist.

THESEUS   We shall never go back to Crete again. You now have another task you can devote yourself to.

ARIADNE   It is not too late.

THESEUS   What do you mean by that?

ARIADNE   As long as you continue to insist you defeated the Minotaur, I shall have to rebel against those lies.

THESEUS   You are far too eager for a fight. There is a time to fight, but there is also a time to surrender to the pleasures of peace. We are not barbarians, after all. It's a virtue of civilisation to know when to desist from fighting. Look, the sun is rising in a cloudless sky. Crete lies beyond the horizon, we are under way to Athens to celebrate our marriage there. Come with me to the lower deck, my companions are longing to see you and to speak to you. But first give me a kiss.

ARIADNE   Kisses cannot change lies into truth.

THESEUS   What a passion for truth in a child of Crete, called the most mendacious land in the world. Why did you bring me that thread, Ariadne?

SCENE 3

The same part of the deck, later. Ariadne is sitting under a canopy of carpets. Theseus is lying in the shade, his head in her lap. He is eating grapes.

THESEUS   I don't understand. Even with this calm we should have been further. We should have seen some islands.

ARIADNE   The sea is sparkling like silver from one horizon to the other.

THESEUS   I have no objection to continuing like this in your company. But don't worry, tomorrow we must see some islands. It can't last much longer. And don't talk about the weather and the view to distract me. You still haven't given me an answer to my question of this morning. Admit it ... you brought me that thread ... because ...

ARIADNE   I don't know.

THESEUS   Confusion and bashfulness suit you better than belligerence. That's how I saw your face the first time when you looked down into the dungeon. So, so, I thought, is that Minos' daughter? She's the prize I want when I've slain the Minotaur.

ARIADNE   Theseus ...

THESEUS   I know what you are going to say. Don't say it now.

ARIADNE   But I must say it.

THESEUS   Have you ever been in the labyrinth?

ARIADNE   I have my conviction.

THESEUS   But I have the experience.

ARIADNE   I don't believe you. I can't believe you.

THESEUS   Listen. I am a king's son. You are a king's daughter. We are born to rule, to make laws and to administer the law, and to make decisions in war and peace. For us the same rules do not apply as for normal people. How could we fulfil our task if we were not halfway between gods and mortals? The king can do anything. The king may not fail. As long as the king shows himself to be superhuman, his power is unassailable. His power lies in the trust of his people.

ARIADNE   You speak like my father. Power, power, power.

THESEUS   King Minos uses his power to make the world afraid,
I want to use my power to bring peace.

ARIADNE   My father found it necessary to invent a monster so
that he could maintain his power on Crete. You are acting, for the
sake of your authority in Athens, as though you have slain that
invented monster. You both want to appear more than you are,
with the aid of something that doesn't exist.

THESEUS   By Zeus, there is no talking to you. What do you
really want? You wanted to destroy the Minotaur. The Minotaur
is destroyed, thanks to me.

ARIADNE   Thanks to you the world will continue to believe there
really was a Minotaur. Who will still dare to doubt it from now on
if Theseus, the great hero, says he slew the Minotaur? And
anyway: it's not a matter of the Minotaur!

THESEUS   Ah, finally we're getting there.

ARIADNE   For me, it's a matter of the truth. I want the truth. I
don't want you to be famous for a deed you did not perform. I
would start to doubt the truth of your other heroic deeds.

THESEUS   Zeus, you wound my honour.

ARIADNE   Nothing is so precious to me as your honour. I shall
be your wife. Your honour is mine. The world stands or falls for
me with your honour. That's why I implore you: admit there was
no Minotaur. Theseus does not need a false pretext to be a hero, a
great king.

THESEUS   Use your intelligence. Athens is in a desperate
situation. Hunger and disease are widespread. Thousands have
fallen in the war, thousands have been taken away as slaves. My
father still wears the crown, but his authority is undermined since
Crete conquered us. Before I sailed away in this ship as a sacrifice
for the Minotaur, my people came lamenting to take leave of me.
'If you are devoured and the king dies, we shall be annexed by
Crete,' they called to me. Then, standing in the bows I swore an
oath: Athens will rise again just as I shall slay the Minotaur! As
we sailed away I heard, from ten thousand throats, my name
sounding over the waves: 'Theseus! Save us! Kill the Minotaur!'

All their hope is centred on me. I alone am capable of giving them courage again, of inspiring them to work hard for the restoration of the city and for the preservation of freedom!

ARIADNE   You can reassure your people and make them happy by coming home with the message: there has never been a Minotaur, and King Minos of Crete has won his victories thanks to lies!

THESEUS   I shall set foot on shore in Athens with the words: I have slain the Minotaur! Athens needs me in the role I have assumed since I was young, that of Theseus, dragon-slayer.

ARIADNE   Oh, don't let me think that you too have only a little soul, Theseus ... to desire the reputation of demi-god!

(She flees to the other end of the deck, and bumps into Phaedra, who is just approaching.)

PHAEDRA   Where is she going? Why is she so pale?

THESEUS   Your sister still doesn't want to believe I killed the Minotaur.

PHAEDRA   Ariadne is strange. She has always been strange. She hears and sees things that aren't there. And she doesn't believe what is there. On Crete she dreamed terrible dreams, night after night. Then she started up shrieking with fear out of her sleep. She recognised you when you came past in the sacrificial procession. It frightened her.

THESEUS   What did she dream about me?

PHAEDRA   She didn't tell me.

THESEUS   Listen, never talk about this, neither on board nor later, in Athens. Theseus' bride has no bad dreams.

PHAEDRA   And then she was always able to get her own way, with my father the king, and with my mother, and with my brothers and our friends ..

THESEUS   And with you? Do you always do what she wants?

PHAEDRA   Sometimes, Sometimes not. That depends. I'm not afraid of my sister.

THESEUS   You say she is strange. Why is she strange?

PHAEDRA   She's not like other girls and women. She doesn't think of the things we like to think about. She doesn't care for beautiful clothes and jewels and perfumes. If I were your bride I would do my best to please you. But Ariadne doesn't even look in the mirror.

THESEUS *(amused)* So, you would want to please me? And how would you do that then, little Phaedra?

PHAEDRA   Oh, I would make myself beautiful. I would dance and sing for you, when you were bored. At table I would fill your goblet. I would read every wish from your eyes even before you had said a word. I would fold your cloak for you ...

THESEUS   What small hands you have.

PHAEDRA   I would be proud of you, because you are the greatest hero in the whole world, and because you slew the Minotaur. I would not allow a single person to doubt it. If I noticed there was such a one on board ... then I would have him thrown to the sharks as a traitor!

THESEUS   Ah, little witch! Without a grain of pity for the poor wretch?

PHAEDRA   Why? You are raised above the judgement of ordinary people. Whoever doubts a prince, or points a finger at him, is assaulting something divine. That is conceit. That can only end in death. It must be so.

THESEUS   What a fire and a pride!

PHAEDRA   I am a princess. I was born and educated to sit on a throne. My father Minos would never have given me to anyone less than a king's son as bridegroom. And I do not intend to be satisfied with less. That's why I don't understand Ariadne. You have chosen her as your wife, and she is still not content. In her place I would be radiant with happiness. I wouldn't contradict you. Your word would be law for me, I would always stand by your side through thick and thin. I would consider it an honour to give your people an example of how to be faithful to the king.

THESEUS   In short, an exemplary consort. But if I wanted to kiss you?

PHAEDRA   If I were your bride, I would open my arms wide, so ... but I am not your bride ...

THESEUS   Tell me, Phaedra, why didn't you bring me that thread in my prison?

PHAEDRA   Ariadne wanted to do it herself.

THESEUS   You have never told me what you think of the Minotaur.

PHAEDRA   The Minotaur is your affair, Theseus. I am only a girl, I don't understand these things. You're a hero, and it's your job to fight monsters. You slew the Minotaur.

THESEUS   Why are you so sure of that?

PHAEDRA   Didn't you say so? What did the Minotaur look like?

THESEUS   You'd have to see him to have any idea of him. He can't be described.

PHAEDRA   But try, Theseus.

THESEUS   He was darkness itself, darkness made visible, tangible. A hot wind blew around him. When he moved, it sounded as though a tempest was raging. He spread a suffocating stink of excrement and blood ...

(Ariadne approaches, not seen by Theseus and Phaedra.)

PHAEDRA   I'd have dropped dead with fear.

THESEUS   He was, as it were, everywhere and nowhere at the same time. He seemed at one moment to swell until he filled the whole cave, and then to shrink into a ball. When I hit out at him with my sword, I struck nothing. Yet I felt his burning breath on my face. He was playing with me like a cat plays with a mouse.

PHAEDRA   Oh!

THESEUS   I knew I was lost if I betrayed fear. So I laughed and loudly challenged him. He was ravenous and rushed at me. But the gods gave me strength. I ...
(He sees Ariadne, who is listening, motionless)
I ... I succeeded in killing him.

PHAEDRA   But how?

THESEUS   Another time. *(calls)* Hey there! Skipper! How does our course stand?

SKIPPER *(approaches)* We must have drifted off course, the ship has got into a current. I swear I don't understand how it happened. Come with me, master, and I'll show you the charts.

(Theseus and Skipper leave.)

ARIADNE   Phaedra, come under the canopy. It's too hot out there in the fierce sun.

PHAEDRA   Now he's gone.

ARIADNE   I didn't ask him to stop.

PHAEDRA   But you don't believe him.

ARIADNE   You don't believe in the Minotaur either, Phaedra.

PHAEDRA   You don't know how to deal with him.

ARIADNE   Must I contribute to him making himself small ... with lies?

PHAEDRA   Oh, they're not lies.

ARIADNE   Boasting is deceit.

PHAEDRA   Aren't all men like that, Ariadne? They like to talk about their heroic deeds, whether they really performed them or not. And if it helps them to feel like heroes and to act like heroes ... why won't you grant them that favour?

ARIADNE   With that indulgence you do them no service.

PHAEDRA   A man who is content with himself can be led.

ARIADNE   I don't want to lead Theseus! I want him to be in control of himself. I want him to be self-confident and purposeful, without false show!

PHAEDRA   But he is the way he is! You can't change him.

ARIADNE   No, I can't change him. He is the only person who can do that. Everyone has that capability: to become what he is not, to grow into a nobler form of himself. It is hard and difficult, it makes heavy demands, it demands sacrifice. But that is life, Phaedra, only that is life!

PHAEDRA   And if Theseus doesn't want to?

ARIADNE   Not to be able to is a misfortune, not to want to is unforgivable.

PHAEDRA   Perhaps he dare not.

ARIADNE   How can I help him more than by constantly spurring him to courage?

PHAEDRA   But instead of making him fall in love you turn him away.

ARIADNE   I only demand the love of the man he could be - if he wants. I wouldn't dare to offer him less than the best of myself.

PHAEDRA   Enjoy what you have, instead of chasing after something that doesn't exist.

ARIADNE   Why do you interfere in this, Phaedra? Why are you trying to make everything that has been achieved fall apart by begging Theseus for tales about the Minotaur?

PHAEDRA   But he is dying to tell them! He wants nothing more than to talk about the Minotaur, to anyone who has ears to hear! I enjoy giving him pleasure.

ARIADNE   Phaedra, little sister, you see him as a big child, because you yourself are still a child.

PHAEDRA   I knew you'd say something like that. I knew you wouldn't listen to my advice.

ARIADNE   Let's not quarrel.

PHAEDRA   Do you remember your bad dream? That dream that keeps coming back? I still remember how you screamed: 'Don't leave me alone! Don't leave me alone!'

ARIADNE   Why are you speaking of that now?

PHAEDRA   Nurse told me that you saw Theseus in that dream.

ARIADNE   I don't know any more what I dreamed.

PHAEDRA   Perhaps that dream was a warning. Didn't our nurse often tell of prophetic dreams, sent to a man to put him on his guard? You are not yet Theseus' wife. He could leave you.

ARIADNE   Theseus would never abandon me.

PHAEDRA   And why not?

ARIADNE   He has given me his word,

PHAEDRA   But Ariadne ... you don't believe his word, when he says he has slain the Minotaur!

ARIADNE   Oh Phaedra!

PHAEDRA   What is it?

ARIADNE   Will you make me doubt Theseus' good faith?

PHAEDRA   Who is doubting Theseus here, you or I? Oh, this heat. Look, the pitch between the planks on the deck is quite soft. How boring it is, all that water, only water, water, nothing but water. Don't you long for trees and mountains and rocks and white houses? How long will it be before we are in Athens?

ARIADNE   I don't know. I heard the skipper say: 'We have drifted off course.' And there is too little wind.

PHAEDRA   If I weren't a princess I would go down to the lower deck and sit with those boys and girls from Athens. At least they're making music, singing and having fun among themselves. Oh look, there's Theseus. He's stopped to talk to them. No wonder he prefers it there. You never leave him in peace for a moment.

ARIADNE   Come, little sister ...

PHAEDRA   Oh, I'm stifling in this heat.

(The Skipper goes past.)

PHAEDRA *(claps her hands)* When will we be in Athens?

SKIPPER   If things stay like this, it may be a long time yet, princess.

PHAEDRA   I want to bathe. Let the girls prepare a bath for me.

SKIPPER   That's impossible, princess, there's not enough water on board.

PHAEDRA   Not enough water?

SKIPPER   If we don't sight an island today or at the latest tomorrow, we'll have to share out drinking water in driblets too, princess.

PHAEDRA   Do you hear that, Ariadne? There's no water! But that's terrible! What shall we do if there's no more water? Oh, I wish I'd never come with you! Isn't Theseus coming?

SKIPPER   Down there they've asked our master to tell more ... about when he laid that monster out cold in the underground cave on your Crete. Would you like more cushions, more carpets? We can bring you anything you want, except water.

ARIADNE Ask Theseus of Athens to come here.

SKIPPER But you see yourself, our master is sitting there in the middle of telling the tale to his companions.

ARIADNE Tell Theseus I want to speak to him.

SKIPPER *(reluctantly)* If you insist ... certainly, princess.

(He spits on the ground as he leaves.)

PHAEDRA You'll see, we'll carry on drifting and drifting without ever seeing land again. Perhaps there'll be a storm as well.

ARIADNE Phaedra, you wanted to run away, not I.

PHAEDRA I'm sick of the heat. The glare of the sea hurts my eyes. You didn't tell me this would be a dangerous voyage. I'm afraid!

ARIADNE Listen, Phaedra ...

PHAEDRA It's all your fault. I hate you, I hate you!

ARIADNE *(shakes her)* Stop it, Phaedra.

THESEUS *(appears on the upper deck)* Let her go. What has she done to you?

PHAEDRA Oh, Theseus! I want to go on land, I want to go on land!

THESEUS I've ordered the skipper to land at the first island we come to, not just to get water but to rest for a whole day. Don't cry, Phaedra. We must come to an island, it must be. You needn't be afraid.

PHAEDRA Oh, Theseus ...

THESEUS *(to Ariadne)* You can't cure anyone's fear with hardness.

ARIADNE Theseus ...

THESEUS Why did you call for me, Ariadne?

ARIADNE Theseus, from now on I will remain silent about the Minotaur. No word of it shall cross my lips any more, as long as I live, I swear to you.

THESEUS You've finally come to your senses. Zeus be praised.

ARIADNE   Promise me then, that you'll never speak of the
     Minotaur again either. Never and nowhere and with no one.
     Promise me that.

THESEUS   How can I promise that? I've explained to you that
     my return, my future, yes, the well-being and honour of the city of
     Athens are inextricably bound to the death of the Minotaur.

ARIADNE   But Theseus, listen ...

THESEUS   Is it starting again? By all the gods and goddesses,
     demons and spirits and whatever else exists between heaven and
     earth, is it all to start again from the beginning!!!?

ARIADNE   I ask for nothing but this: that you respect the truth.

THESEUS   I wish I'd never seen you.

SKIPPER *(comes running)* Master! Master! Land ahoy!

THESEUS   At last.

SKIPPER   Still just a streak, master, a mark on the horizon. But
     it's one of the Cyclades; it fits in with my reckoning.

THESEUS   What's the island called?

SKIPPER   If I'm not mistaken ... Naxos!

ACT THREE

SCENE 1

A clearing among rocks and bushes, on the island of Naxos.
Theseus is sitting with his head in his hands, on a stone. The
Skipper comes in search of him.

SKIPPER   Master, why didn't you come hunting with us?

THESEUS   Leave me, I didn't feel like it today.

SKIPPER   We haven't seen you happy for one moment.

THESEUS   That will pass.

SKIPPER   They say that princess of Crete, the oldest of the two,
     I mean, has the evil eye.

THESEUS   Oh, superstition.

SKIPPER   The crew think it's her fault there hasn't been a
     favourable wind to Athens.

THESEUS   The princess is my bride. I will not tolerate her being spoken of in this tone on board.

SKIPPER   Yes, master. But you know how people are. The princess is beautiful, and virtuous, it's true. But she's still a foreigner. Those Cretans are strange people. You don't know where you are with them.

THESEUS   That's for me alone to judge.

SKIPPER   Of course, master. I beg your forgiveness. It will probably all change in good time. Now take that other princess, the little one. She was just watching the games on the beach. She laughed and clapped her hands and gave a silver clasp from her hair to the winner. You see, the fellows like that sort of thing.

THESEUS   Where is Ariadne?

SKIPPER   I don't know, master. Master, you will be coming now to have a look at the game we have shot? You must let people see that you are well.

THESEUS   Do they think I'm ill, then?

SKIPPER   You're not yourself. Whoever has eyes to see and ears to hear knows that.

THESEUS   It's nothing.

SKIPPER   Master, they don't understand why you don't want to talk about your fight with the monster in the labyrinth. They're still waiting for an account of what happened. You promised, but when it comes to talking, you look for a way out. They're not used to that from you. It confuses people. They wonder what's going on. The Minotaur has been slain, hasn't he, master?

THESEUS   Does anyone dare to doubt it?

SKIPPER   No, master, but it's strange you don't want to talk about it.

THESEUS   Rest assured, and assure the others too, I shall speak of it.

(Ariadne approaches over the rocks.)

SKIPPER   When then, master? Right now, at the meal? The perfect time! That will give us fresh courage for the rest of the voyage.

THESEUS *(sees Ariadne)* No, tomorrow. Tomorrow I shall tell the men how I slew the Minotaur.

SKIPPER   As you wish, master. But you mustn't put it off too long. It's not good when people start muttering among themselves ... about something that should really be a foregone conclusion. *(moves away)*

THESEUS *(to Ariadne)* You hear that. I couldn't allow myself to remain silent, even if I wanted to. You don't have the right to demand that of me.

ARIADNE   If you can't remain silent, then tell them the truth!

THESEUS   You must know that is impossible!

ARIADNE   Theseus! So you're finally admitting there was no Minotaur?

THESEUS   Is it just a matter of hearing that from my mouth? You win, Ariadne. You win. If that's the price I must pay for my peace, good, I'm ready to say it here as often as you want: there was no Minotaur. There has never been a Minotaur!

ARIADNE   I don't want you to say it for my sake.

THESEUS   Are you still not satisfied? I've finally said you were right. What more, in the name of whatever you want, can you still demand of me?

ARIADNE   I want you to say it because you can't do otherwise, because it's the truth.

THESEUS   You're asking the impossible. Now I've said what you were desperate to hear, I consider the question settled, for good. This remains between you and me. I expect of you that you won't oppose me from now on. More, that as the bride of Theseus of Athens, you will support me, when the Minotaur is talked of.

ARIADNE   When ... what?

THESEUS   When I judge it necessary to tell whoever, wherever, how I slew the Minotaur.

ARIADNE   Then will you still continue to maintain that, in spite of everything?

THESEUS   Tomorrow I tell my travelling companions and the crew the story they demand and that they have a right to: how I killed the Minotaur, and you will not oppose me.

ARIADNE   Before you speak, I'll tell them the truth.

THESEUS   I'll set my word against yours.

ARIADNE   I was born and raised on Crete. As long as I remember I have lived in the shadow of the Minotaur, have seen the shadow grow black and threatening over the island and over the people who live on it. Oh, you haven't heard, as a child, that drumroll in the silent streets, when the annual offerings were chosen. The most beautiful girls, the strongest young men. No one dared complain or protest ....was it not an honour to be devoured by the god? Mothers who dared to scream, fathers who raised their fists, ran the risk of being arrested by the high priest and his servants for treason and sacrilege. Parents didn't rejoice any more when they had fine, healthy children. Food for the god! The Minotaur ruled everything, the state, the family, work, thoughts. He was the giver and the taker, he was the beginning and the end. My father issued orders in his name. I wasn't surprised when I noticed that on Crete people were afraid of silence, of being alone, of thinking. Thinking is dangerous, thinking leads to asking questions. At the bull games and singing and dancing people don't start thinking. There was always plenty of entertainment on Crete. Scarcely was one festival over, than my father announced another one. No wonder: it was important for him that no-one thought. It's his misfortune that I was born with a passion for that forbidden, dangerous thinking. When my brothers wanted to know too much, my father sent them away, or he punished them, or he distracted them with banquets and vanity. He saw no danger in me. Daughters are toys, decoration, they don't actually count. My father encouraged my understanding, just as someone urges on a lapdog to perform tricks. But thinking is a fire that spreads rapidly, everything is food for thought. I saw and I heard, and the more I saw and heard, the more I loathed the Minotaur. I hated him because he forced us into degrading slavery. I thought of means to fight him, to destroy him. But I realised I had to keep silent about my ideas. For when I looked around me, I saw how perfectly my father's system worked: our armies conquered everything and everyone, wealth flowed into Crete, the world lay at our feet. I saw that people forgot the price they had to pay for glory, honour and prosperity. They were drunk with ambition and pride, and praised the god to the heavens, especially when my father had human sacrifices come from the conquered lands. Then I couldn't bear it any longer. Think of that, Theseus: my world was permeated with the Minotaur, through and through. I was conscious of the Minotaur awake and in dreams, I was possessed by the Minotaur, and I knew that on Crete all the others, high and low, were in the same state as I ... and then suddenly I hear from the mouth of my father, King Minos, the highest in the land, who made laws and directed the ritual for the Minotaur: 'There is no Minotaur, and there has never been one, for I, Minos, invented the Minotaur ... for power, for power!' The power to subject the world to him with bragging and bluff! And the people put up with it! They forget they are born with the capacity to think. They barter their own judgement for chimeras, lies and high-sounding phrases, for games and bread! For the glory of their country, that rests on violence and deceit, they take pride in the favour of their god in the labyrinth, they call themselves a chosen people! When I heard the truth, I swore an oath: to raise my voice. To join battle. Everywhere and always. Against the Minotaur. Against every lie created to confuse people's judgement, that hinders them from thinking for themselves. Woe betide me, Theseus, if against my better judgement I should betray the truth.

THESEUS   But I ask nothing more of you than that you remain silent.

ARIADNE   Silence is collusion. If I, by keeping silent, support you in your story of the fight with the Minotaur, I'm promoting the existence of a Minotaur on earth. I'm helping to encourage people in the delusion that there was a Minotaur, that there could sometime, somewhere still be a Minotaur. Don't you understand that I won't, can't, may not do that? I live to deny the Minotaur and everything that resembles him.

THESEUS   Ariadne, for my sake ...

ARIADNE   For no one's sake.

THESEUS   You only think of yourself.

ARIADNE   Yes! I am thinking of myself. I am, because I have a conscience. To renounce that is for me non-being, death.

THESEUS   Are you going to carry on like this opposing everything that doesn't fit in with that conscience of yours?

ARIADNE   Yes, that's the way it is.

THESEUS   So I can expect war without end between you and me?

ARIADNE   We don't always have to be opponents!

THESEUS   As ruler and leader, in the interests of my people I shall more than once have to undertake measures that in your eyes might appear to be deceit.

ARIADNE   Why is that necessary?

THESEUS   Without it no authority can exist of one over many.

ARIADNE   That is to condemn authority.

THESEUS   You are either very stupid or very dangerous.

ARIADNE   Those are the words of Minos. When he said that, I read my death sentence in his look.

THESEUS   That should have warned you to be careful.

ARIADNE   I've entered on a course in which there is no turning back.

THESEUS   What have I let myself in for!

ARIADNE   If that is so, if you're reluctant to make me your wife, then let me go.

THESEUS   That's impossible. You've saved my life, I've given you my word. In the presence of the people on board I called you my bride. No-one shall ever be able to say of Theseus that he breaks his word.

ARIADNE   Then let me take my own freedom back.

THESEUS   So that the whole world knows that Theseus of Athens is spurned by a woman? Out of the question!

ARIADNE   Then there's no other solution than that we learn to tolerate one another.

(Phaedra and Skipper enter.)

SKIPPER   Master, the hunters are back on the shore, they're waiting for you, to inspect the spoils and to choose the offerings for the sea gods ...

(Theseus leaves quickly along the rock path.)

PHAEDRA   Why is he going away now? I was looking for him. He promised me I might lead the dance with him, after the sacrifice. *(to Ariadne)* Why has he gone away? Can't you talk to Theseus just once without making him angry!

SKIPPER   I'm going to my master.

PHAEDRA   It's your fault he's forgotten that promise. You always spoil everything. You always come between us. You won't let me have him for a moment. I'm sure you're afraid I'll take him away from you.

ARIADNE   You don't know what you're saying.

PHAEDRA   Perhaps you don't believe I could take him away from you if I wanted?

ARIADNE   Oh, Phaedra.

PHAEDRA   You don't believe it. You think I'm just joking. A childish joke.

ARIADNE   Of course that's what I think.

PHAEDRA   Has Theseus ever asked you to lead the dance with him?

ARIADNE   He knows you like dancing and that you were bored on the ship.

PHAEDRA   Oh, you think he's providing a little amusement for the poor little child on Naxos?

ARIADNE   Don't be a fool, Phaedra.

PHAEDRA   I'm not a fool. You're the fool. Only a fool would gamble away her happiness like you. I'd never be such a fool.

ARIADNE   I wanted to free Theseus from his promise to marry me.

PHAEDRA   Did you say that to him?

ARIADNE   Theseus keeps to his word, and he won't tolerate any breach of faith from me.

PHAEDRA   But he doesn't love you! And you don't love him!

ARIADNE   There's more at stake for us than love.

PHAEDRA   If you felt love for one another you wouldn't quarrel about the Minotaur.

ARIADNE   No love is possible until we are at one over the Minotaur.

PHAEDRA   Ah, that love of yours is unworldly and supernatural! Theseus is only a man.

ARIADNE   Theseus wants to be more than a man. His ambition reaches half way to the gods.

PHAEDRA   But you want to be godlike in your pride.

ARIADNE   The truth applies to gods and humans.

PHAEDRA   Is that truth more important for you than anything else?

ARIADNE   For me it is as indispensable as the air I breathe.

PHAEDRA   Is truth the only thing for you? Tell me, would you never be lonely, never unhappy, never uncertain ... even if you were sitting, say, on an uninhabited island? Completely alone and forsaken? Ariadne, would you still place truth above everything else then?

ARIADNE   I don't know. How can I know that? I'm a human being, I live among human beings. No-one is ever completely alone ... on an uninhabited island.

PHAEDRA   This is an uninhabited island, Ariadne.

ARIADNE   You are with me. And we are not alone either.

PHAEDRA   Do you hear the music? Those Athenians are dancing on the shore. Will you come with me to watch?

ARIADNE   No, I'm tired.

PHAEDRA   You don't care for dancing, and you've quarrelled with Theseus.

ARIADNE   The grass is soft, here under the trees.
     (She lies down.)

PHAEDRA   You didn't sleep much on board. When I opened my eyes in the night, I saw you standing at the bulwarks. Or you were

walking up and down the deck. Why? Didn't you dare to sleep,
because you were afraid you'd dream again about: Don't leave me
alone, don't leave me alone!

ARIADNE *(half asleep)* No, Phaedra, I won't leave you alone, I'll
stay here with you.

PHAEDRA *(walking around)* Look, down there on the shore they've
lit the torches. The sun is setting. They're busy roasting meat.
I've sent the girls to gather pomegranates and grapes and figs, as
many as they can carry, to take with us on board. I don't intend to
go thirsty again, if there's another water shortage. I wish we were
already in Athens. Ariadne? Are you asleep?
(She comes up close)
You're really asleep. But you're not dreaming. Your face is as
peaceful as the sea in a calm. Why aren't you dreaming? Because
you aren't afraid any more? Because you are certain? Because
you're happy, with that truth of yours, that you love so
passionately that you forget to be a woman? So you don't want to
have Theseus? Oh, but I do want him, totally, all mine, mine alone
... Why aren't you dreaming? Dream, Ariadne, dream ... of
Theseus, who doesn't desire you. No, not of Theseus, dream
rather of the Minotaur ... of the Minotaur. Why do you keep
saying he doesn't exist? Oh, how you must believe in the
Minotaur to be able to hate him as you do ...

*(Theseus goes past along the rock path. Phaedra starts and
leaps forward..)*

PHAEDRA   Theseus! I am afraid. It's so dark.
THESEUS   No wonder you're trembling. This is a lonely place,
especially after sunset. Where's –
PHAEDRA *(quickly)* There's a smell of wine about you.
THESEUS *(laughs)* Yes, the wine is sweet and cool and flows like
water. Come and drink with me, little Phaedra.
PHAEDRA   I am thirsty. And you've promised me we shall lead
the boys and girls of Athens in the dance.

THESEUS   We shall forget everything and be joyful. One carefree night on the island of Naxos I might really grant myself, before I ...

PHAEDRA   Ouch!

THESEUS   What is it?

PHAEDRA   My foot! I tripped over a stone. I think I can't walk any more.

THESEUS   Then I shall carry you.

PHAEDRA   I'm heavy.

THESEUS   Not heavier than my little son Hippolytus.

PHAEDRA   He's a child. Do you mean by that that I'm a child too?

THESEUS   You, Phaedra? No, you're not a child.

PHAEDRA   Put me down, Theseus. What would Ariadne say?

THESEUS   That's true, but it's you I want to hold in my arms.

PHAEDRA   There's not room for both of us. You have to choose between me and Ariadne.

THESEUS   I'm no longer free to choose.

PHAEDRA   Must I live in Athens in your palace beside you and Ariadne ... as your little sister? Or as the sister of your little son Hippolytus?

THESEUS   Damn it, Phaedra.

PHAEDRA   Or do you intend to seek a bridegroom for me ... noble enough for my rank, and strong enough to lift me up in his arms ... as you just did?

(Theseus embraces her, she allows it, then breaks free.)

Ariadne stands between us.

THESEUS   Yes, between you and me. Between me and myself.

PHAEDRA   Between you and the Minotaur.

THESEUS   That too, that above all: between me and the Minotaur.

PHAEDRA   Oh, I understand you so well. You are a hero. You have a right to the Minotaur. No-one may deny you that right. Whoever does so must realise he's risking his life.

THESEUS   Listen, Phaedra, it's because I am a hero ... that there are certain things I cannot do, ever.

PHAEDRA   Of course. You couldn't do what my father Minos does ... when someone thwarts him.

THESEUS   Impossible. I'm not a barbarian.

PHAEDRA   If I were Ariadne ... oh, then I wouldn't want to stand in your way. If I saw that I was a stumbling block for you, and that you didn't love me ... then without further ado I'd throw myself from the rocks. But I know my sister Ariadne. She'd never do anything like that. Never. She'd never doubt herself. She won't give up what she's set her mind on. She is strong, Ariadne, stronger than you think. Your happiness, or her happiness, that is unimportant for her, as long as she has her truth to live for. Yes, she'd even die out of love for that truth, if she had to but never for you or me ...

THESEUS   I know. Fate has willed it so.

PHAEDRA   Sail to Athens without me. I'll stay here on Naxos.

THESEUS   You don't know what you're saying. This is an inhospitable island, where no people live.

PHAEDRA   But I don't want to live.

THESEUS   You mustn't sacrifice yourself, Phaedra.

PHAEDRA   But what then, what then?

THESEUS   I must learn to look at you without seeing you, learn to hear what you say without listening to the sound of your voice. I must avoid your company.

PHAEDRA   Must that really be so?

THESEUS   There is no other solution for a man of honour.

PHAEDRA *(throws herself in his arms)* Theseus! ... Can't you see you can't pretend I don't exist!

SKIPPER *(beckoning from behind the rocks)* Master, master! The wind is rising, a fine wind, in the right direction! A wind blowing straight to Athens! If we want to take advantage of it, we must hoist the sails straight away! You must come on board, master, the others are all on board, the crew's ready!

THESEUS   Poseidon be thanked! Come, Phaedra.

SKIPPER   A stroke of luck, that wind. The offerings we made today to the sea gods have certainly been well received. May Poseidon carry on favouring us, and make this weather last a few days. Tomorrow we can be on Delos. We can't ignore this gift, master, we've no time to lose.

THESEUS   I'm coming. Come with me, Phaedra.

PHAEDRA   I hate that wind, that won't give me a few hours alone with you!

THESEUS   We must set sail, Phaedra.

SKIPPER   Master, we're only waiting for you and for the two princesses from Crete.

THESEUS   Ariadne isn't here.

SKIPPER   I haven't seen the princess anywhere.

THESEUS   Then we must look for her.

PHAEDRA *(quickly)* My sister was tired, she wanted to sleep. She's already on board.

THESEUS *(calling to the Skipper)* She's already on board!

SKIPPER   Hurry then, master. Every moment counts.

THESEUS   Let's go.

PHAEDRA *(tense)* What do you see ... Theseus?

(As he tries to drag Phaedra with him, he notices the look she casts behind her. He sees, under the bushes, the hem of the dress of the sleeping Ariadne. Phaedra and Theseus stare at one another silently. There is a moment of tension, a silent battle between the two. Theseus yields.)

THESEUS   The moon shining on the bushes.

SKIPPER   On board! On board!

(Theseus picks up Phaedra and follows the Skipper.)

SCENE 3

Moonlight moves to the place where Ariadne is sleeping, and shines into her face.

ARIADNE *(waking up)* What did you say, Phaedra? I'm sorry, I
didn't understand what you said. I fell asleep. I was so tired ...
Phaedra? Phaedra! Where are you, Phaedra? It's night, the moon
is shining, they're not singing any more down there on the shore.

(She stands up and runs a little way between the rocks)

 Where are the torches, the fires? Oh, the ship! The ship is sailing
away! Wait for me! Don't sail away without me. Don't leave me
alone! Oh, Theseus! Phaedra! Don't leave me alone!

(She sinks down on a rock.)

*(In the distance the sound is heard of cymbals and singing voices
and dancing footsteps. In an unearthly light there stands
suddenly, young and radiant, crowned with vines, wrapped in a
leopardskin, the god Dionysos.)*

DIONYSOS   Don't grieve!
    A handsome arabesque is your despair.
    Yet you could make a thousand more,
    As handsome, less mournful certainly.
    With arms upraised and unbound hair sing 'Evoé!'
    The unbridled dance call of my retinue.
ARIADNE   This is no man that speaks to me.
DIONYSOS   I am the divine intoxication, comforter supreme of the
    forsaken.
ARIADNE   I am forsaken because I want the truth.
DIONYSOS   The truth is an invention of mortals.
    For among the gods nothing is true, nothing untrue.
    There things are rounded off, completely one.
    Only a mortal sets one thing against the other,
    Marshalls all he knows
    In good and evil, black and white,
    In light and darkness, and so on.
    There is a Minotaur, Ariadne, and there is none.

Drink divine wine with me, and wear my wreath,
Free yourself from the dichotomy
That dwells relentless in all earthly things
And be immortal in my paradise,
Where, shadowless, nothing has opposite.

ARIADNE   I'm not of your sphere, I am a mortal.

DIONYSOS   See, where I am all is ripe and full,
The earth burns under fiery dancing feet.
The grapes burst on the laden vine.
Who meets with me feels frenzy in the blood,
And madly beats cymbal and tambourine.
So dance with us, join my triumphal march!
A god makes her divine, who him enchants.
I feel your sorrows and your deep distress,
Through chaste pride made infinitely sweet ...
Courageous and cool, you tempt me, Ariadne.
Perhaps I am the god you secretly adore.

ARIADNE   I have never called on a god, I expect no help from
gods.

DIONYSOS   Believe, and be reborn in my carousing!

ARIADNE   You throw no shadow. You're of a different kind.
For me you don't exist.

DIONYSOS   Give me your hand, the difference will vanish.
Step from the human world into the light of gods.
Sing: 'Evoé!' No loneliness, no pain,
And what you name the truth is meaningless.

ARIADNE   Then I'll stay here. I'd rather be alone and suffer
pain in a world where the truth has meaning.

DIONYSOS   Here are no people. All have fled in a fast ship,
beyond the horizon, away from your truth which does not hold for
them. Put aside your human consciousness. It is like your
shadow: light and darkness, elusive, fleeting, a deceiving nought.

ARIADNE   Lead me not into temptation. I *will* not.

DIONYSOS   There is no path, no golden middle path between the
way of gods and that of mortals.

ARIADNE   There is, along the razor's edge.

DIONYSOS   And there you wish to walk? That is more than pride:
a challenge to eternal nature!

ARIADNE   I challenge it! I live for that! For that I am a human!

DIONYSOS   What is a human, alone, and without other humans?
Dare think it, Ariadne: death ...

ARIADNE *(in the full realisation of her fate)* Death ...? Death!
(runs to the rocks) The ship is gone! There's nothing more to be
seen. Oh Theseus, Phaedra! Don't leave me alone!

*(In despair she throws herself down on the place where she had
been lying asleep)*

Don't leave me alone!

DIONYSOS   I take delight in you, and therefore I give you the
rarest gift of the gods: to go back three days in your human time,
to live three days, a chance for a new choice, consciousness
feeding on memory. Oh, regal good fortune: a different fate!

*(The light fades, the landscape disappears in darkness. The
grass verge on which Ariadne is lying, seems to be the couch in
her room in Knossos. She throws herself from one side to the
other, caught in the oppression of her dream. The Nurse and
Phaedra enter. The Nurse is carrying clothes over her arm.)*

PHAEDRA   Sister! Ariadne! What is it, what's the matter with
you?

NURSE   She's dreaming. Wake her up *(to herself)* Again the
same, always the same; this is a bad omen.

PHAEDRA   Ariadne! Open your eyes.

ARIADNE *(still half in the dream)* Don't leave me alone!

PHAEDRA   But I'm here. I'm with you. Wake up. You're
dreaming, Ariadne.

ARIADNE   A dream? *(still trembling)* That dream was more
tangible than reality. Oh Phaedra!

(Ariadne compulsively clings on to her sister.)

PHAEDRA   But what did you dream?

NURSE   Here's your tunic, your veil. Let me tie your sandals.

PHAEDRA   Hurry up, Ariadne, they're waiting for us. The ship from Athens has been in the harbour since sunrise. I saw the victims coming on to the quay.

NURSE   Seven beautiful girls, seven strapping young men.

PHAEDRA   Fairer and sturdier than us Cretans.

NURSE   Fourteen lives in their prime for our god in the labyrinth. Oh, he will smile on us this year.

PHAEDRA   The son of the King of Athens is among them, as promised. He himself is fair as a god.

NURSE   Did you see him?

PHAEDRA   The victims went past under my window, on their way to the temple. He was walking in front of the others. Do you hear the crowd cheering outside? Hurry, Ariadne, they'll be arriving. *(at the window)* Yes, you see, they've been consecrated, the victims, they're wearing white tunics and wreaths on their heads.

ARIADNE   Oh, my dream!

NURSE   Hush, child, that is over now.

ARIADNE   No, it is beginning ...

PHAEDRA   Come, we're expected at the banquet.

ARIADNE   I don't want to celebrate, I can't. Where is my father?

NURSE   King Minos is speaking in the throne room with the High Priest. He's preparing himself for the sacrifice.

ARIADNE   That sacrifice is not going to take place. I shall prevent it. The Minotaur ...

NURSE   Hush! How dare you name the name of our god so loudly.

ARIADNE   He is not my god, the Minotaur.

NURSE   Come to your senses. You're dreaming. You're still dreaming.

ARIADNE   No, I am wide awake.

NURSE *(clinging to Ariadne's knees, to prevent her from going)*
    Child, my child, be sensible. Think of your dream.
ARIADNE   Yes, I am thinking of my dream.

(Frees herself from her nurse and slowly walks towards the door)

NURSE   Where are you going?
ARIADNE   To Naxos.

Hella Haasse

Born in Djakarta, she spent her early years in the Dutch East Indies.
She trained at drama school and has written several plays, novellas,
autobiographies, essays and poems but it is for her novels that she is
best known. Since the publication of her novel, *Urug* which was filmed
in 1993, she has been widely recognised. She has won numerous
literary prizes, including the Constantijn Huygens Prize in 1987 and the
P.C. Hooft prize in 1983.

Translated titles include:

The Scarlet City. (Academy Chicago)
In a Dark Wood Wandering. (Hutchinson)
Forever a stranger. (Oxford in Asia Press)
Threshold of Fire. (Academy Chicago)

EAT

by Matin van Veldhuizen
translated by Rina Vergano

Dutch premiere: 19th September 1991 in de Toneelschuur
in Haarlem, the Netherlands.
Director: Matin van Veldhuizen

CHARACTERS

Bea Trudy de Jong
Jo Ditha van der Linden
Anna Lineke Rijxman

Bea and Anna's house.
The anniversary of their mother's death.
The three sisters drink wine continually throughout the performance.

BEA I'm worn out .... finished.
 (looks at her watch)
 they'll be here soon, Jo and Anna and I've had it.
 I'm worn out, spent, finished, dead beat
 all those questions
 all those answers
 all that being nice, obliging, pleasant
 I'm tired of all those people, tired of all those eyes,
 tired of all those mouths
 I haven't got any more answers
 they're finished, finished, finished
 I want to be alone
 not see anyone
 not hear anyone
 I want to be at home

tired and empty of questions and answers
at home
as fast as possible
alone
and eat, eat, eat
she sees herself tearing along ...
no-one can stop her
not even me
like a misty film
in which she herself is playing
the repulsive starring role
in a horrible film
driven by panic
she does what she has to do
like all those times before.
she does what she has to do
she is stronger than I am
I can only see her driven by hunger
she runs into the supermarket
wrenches a trolley out of the line
starts grabbing at food
loading it in
everything, everything, everything
it doesn't matter what
she piles it up
until it's completely full
of that which is edible
then she pays the bill, impatiently
with obvious haste
she pays the bill
she wants to be home
alone
alone with her best friend
with her biggest enemy
alone with her secret
en route she bites open

the plastic wrapping
of a soft flabby package
it is wet, cold
still half-frozen
chopped raw meat
I read quickly
cubed chicken, 500 grammes
she takes a handful
stuffs it into her mouth
and without chewing
swallows it
takes another handful
and another
I see
how she feels the cold hard pieces
sliding into her stomach
almost home
and then
on the blue lino
of the kitchen floor
everything's spread out
deep-freeze vegetables, peanuts,
pizzas, cakes, raw liver,
blocks of butter, custard, yoghurt,
tins of beans, peaches, cat food.
she cannot wait
time is short
madness has struck
she shovels everything down her throat
everything she must
she cannot avoid it
I see
her smeared face
her lumpy hair
her clothes full of stains
I cannot believe my eyes

all the food has vanished
bottles, jars,
empty tins, cartons,
are all that's left
then I feel my stomach
my over-stuffed stomach
my heavily pregnant stomach
and I drink ...
water, water, water
a bit later
when I'm down on my knees
on the bath mat
I vomit it all up
all that poison
all the colours and shapes still intact
and I see
through my tearful eyes
and my wet fingers
that she has given birth to the devil
empty, relieved and exhausted
I feel disgust, revulsion,
guilt
I despise myself
hate myself deeply
I'll never do this again
god, let me never do this again
never again
I'm worn out ... finished
(Bea looks at her watch)
they'll be here soon Jo and Anna
and I've had it
*(She turns the television on, feels the soil of the one plant in the
room, mumbles)*
bloody hell
*(She hears Anna arriving home, picks up an aerosol can and
sprays, pretends to watch the TV. Anna enters. She sniffs the*

scent of the aerosol, lights a cigarette, pours wine for Bea and
herself)

ANNA   what's eating you? have you been crying?

BEA   I don't know what's wrong

ANNA   what's wrong then?

BEA   it's enough to make me weep
it's all enough to make me weep
I only have to turn the TV on
and wham!
someone's winning money
in some wretched quiz
wham
terrible
chat shows for young christians
the Little House on the Prairie
a bloody children's film would you believe
wham, like a ballcock
the news

ANNA   that always makes you laugh

BEA   films about failed relationships
families which fall apart
and when it's all patched up
wham
nature films
films about animals

ANNA   Ed, the talking horse
(sings) a horse is a horse
d'you remember?

BEA *(crying)* of course, of course

ANNA   and nobody talks to a horse of course
unless the horse of course of course
is the famous Mr Ed
(Anna toasts her, pours more wine)
here drink
sentimental fool

BEA   the slightest thing

and I'm brimming over
ANNA   you're emotionally unstable
you work far too hard
was it busy again at the exhibition
BEA   yes but it's not that
ANNA   what is it then?
is it because Jo's coming
is it today
BEA   I've had it for days
weeks, months
I've got hot flushes
I'm regularly troubled by hot flushes
ANNA   you can't be
not for ages yet
BEA   it does happen with some types of people
ANNA   yes with women
but it's an exception at your age
BEA   and I stink
ANNA   nonsense
if you stank
I would have told you right away
you know that
(silence)
where do you stink then?
BEA   all over the place
in every intimate place I smell
an unfresh fragrance of jungle flowers
and feel sure I'm dirty
ANNA   it's probably just stress
stress odour from working too hard
animals have that too
BEA   animals?
stress odour from working too hard
ANNA   go to the zoo for the day
then you'll smell it
BEA   keepers, they work

animals do nothing

ANNA   oh, Bea be happy
that you stink in the wild
and not behind bars

BEA   I do stink then
you said it

ANNA   you smell nice, really
you always smell nice
I couldn't do without your stench
(She puts her arm around Bea)

BEA   you haven't watered *the* plant this morning

ANNA   forgot sorry
I hate plants
and certainly *the* plant
I haven't got green fingers like you

BEA   you don't need green fingers
to water a plant
jesus Anna
we've got one plant

ANNA   *you've* got one plant
that's one plant too many in this house

BEA   does the plant bother you?

ANNA   yes

BEA   don't be so ridiculous

ANNA   *it* stinks
you don't stink
that plant stinks

BEA   of what?

ANNA   of everything that's dirty
let's get rid of it

BEA   no
over my dead body
I've had that plant since he was a cutting
from ... from childhood on
I've looked after that plant, pampered him
I've reared him

ANNA *(horrified)* reared?

BEA   yes reared
   I've reared him with love that plant
   (She starts snivelling again)

ANNA   alright Bea, alright
   he can stay
   *(Jo enters with a plant and bottles of wine. She looks ravishing,
   sniffs the aerosol scent.)*

JO   who smells so nice in here?

ANNA   Bea

BEA   our plant

ANNA   we do

JO   delightful
   who can stay, Frank?
   how is Frank

ANNA   Adrian

JO   Adrian
   no Frank

ANNA   no not Frank
   Adrian

JO   Frank, you mean
   he was called Frank
   (Exit Bea)

ANNA   Frank was last year
   the current one's called Adrian
   Frank always wore scary socks

JO   Adrian Adrian
   what a godawful name
   what's the matter with Bea?
   has she been crying

ANNA   just a bit over-worked
   she's doing the ideal home exhibition
   and she's being driven mad by
   all those awful people and their endless moaning
   leave her
   she'll be all right in a bit

fancy some wine?

JO   yes love some

(Anna pours the wine. Bea enters beaming. She has smartened herself up)

BEA   what a gorgeous plant Jo
lovely isn't it Anna

ANNA   isn't it

JO   lovely eh
now you've got one each
one plant is so pathetic

ANNA   that plant isn't pathetic
he's been reared with a lot of love

JO   reared? cultivated

ANNA   no reared

BEA   yes reared
how are Vincent and Rose

JO   very well
they send their love and a kiss from Rose

BEA   not from Vincent

ANNA   Vincent isn't the kissy type
fortunately

JO   not with everyone
fortunately but you'd be surprised

ANNA   oh really, do tell

JO   since when
were you interested in kissing?

BEA   Anna is writing an article about sex
for a French magazine
sex in Europe

ANNA   women and sex in Europe

JO *(to Anna) you* writing about sex

ANNA   *me* yes
that's my profession you know
writing

JO   yes I know that
but about sex, *you*

ANNA   you've put on weight
JO   no I haven't
BEA   she's as slim as anything
   (To Jo) stand up
   (Jo stands up) oh yes, you have put on weight
BEA   a little fuller in the face at most
JO   oh no
ANNA   oh yes
   your thighs are touching again
   I can see it
JO   impossible
   I'm very careful with food
   I don't weigh any more
   than I did last year
ANNA   are you still doing weightwatchers?
   that word
   weightwatchers
   birdwatchers that's understandable
   but weightwatchers ... weightwatchers
   losing weight in a group
   collective fat control
   with surveillance
JO   you'd rather starve alone
   until you're as light as a feather
   and leave us carrying the can
ANNA   rather that
   than thighs which slap together
JO   slapping thighs are better
   than one of those great gaps in between
   like the Eiffel Tower
   (Bea is on the edge of tears again)
BEA   let's not start talking about the Eiffel Tower
   and things like that
   dammit
   Jo hasn't been here five minutes
   and it's already going downhill

dammit
why have we come together?
let's drink *(raises her glass, looks up)*
cheers! to mother!

JO   to mother!

ANNA   to mother!
sorry mum but Jo was asking for it
(toasts) hope you're having a good time

JO   yeh

ANNA *(to Bea)* mother is reunited with your father once more

JO   an idiotic idea

BEA   do you think they sell cake in heaven?

JO   cake must be free up there

ANNA   let them eat cake
do you think they were happy Bea?
you never say anything about your father

BEA   there isn't much to say
I was still so young when he died
I was just six
one year later
I had a new father
and shortly after that
Jo was born
I remember that as clear as a bell
I was staying with granny and grandad
and when I went back
I was going to have a little brother or sister
in the kitchen
I heard grandad saying to granny
it isn't a child
it's a rabbit
it's all long and thin
and it's got huge ears
it doesn't even weigh five pounds
I was terribly happy
what a surprise

I was getting a rabbit
instead of a little brother or sister
(to Jo) god, what a disappointment
when I saw you lying there in that crib
JO   weren't you happy to see me?
BEA   I'd have preferred a rabbit
ANNA   before she got that brace
she did have those ...
JO   you're off your rocker
ANNA   anything else to get off your chest
weightwatcher
BEA   he chomped
dammit he chomped
mother always said
Albert, you're chomping again
Bea, he's chomping again
can you hear him?
and he didn't even have false teeth
I always felt sorry for him
he couldn't help it, that chomping
you chomp or you don't chomp
mother couldn't stand it
she had her ears pricked
at every meal
I did too
I prayed to god that he wouldn't chomp
ANNA   our mother had taste
when it came to men
I must admit
BEA   I can still hear him chomping
ANNA   a horse is a horse
BEA/JO/ANNA of course of course
BEA *(toasts)* to mother!
ANNA   to mother!
JO   to mother!
what are we eating anyway Bea?

ANNA   are you allowed to eat with those thighs

BEA   we're going out to eat

ANNA   out?

    you were going to cook

BEA   I know

    but I didn't have time

    to do any shopping

    it was so busy at the exhibition

    I was too late to do any shopping

    I thought

    I won't cook then

    we'll drink something here

    and then I'll take them out to eat

    more festive

ANNA   festive

    on a day like today

JO   festive

    I hadn't bargained on that

BEA   borrow something of Anna's then

ANNA   too small

    won't fit

JO   I don't wear children's clothes anyway

ANNA   put one of Bea's skirts on

    at least it'll hide those chafing thighs

BEA   and he was mad about legs

ANNA   who?

BEA   my father

    he was mad about women's legs

    he always looked at legs

    why isn't that Doreen married?

    she's got a good enough undercarriage

    he used to call women with beautiful legs

    doggies

    here look at that little doggie

    me too

    I always looked at women's legs

when I sat on the back of his bike
I'd shout
look dad, what a doggie!
and still
I still notice women's legs
fortunately he didn't live to see mine
go to the dogs
JO   mother had very beautiful legs
BEA   yes, he adored her
he bent over backwards for that woman
ANNA   mother was a complete beauty
JO   until she got ill
BEA   you two should have seen her then
she was very beautiful
a very striking appearance
when I walked along the street with her
men used to whistle at her
do you remember Jo
when I said that to your father
because I was so proud of her
he was furious
and said that was common, whistling
and that if you got whistled at
it was because you were asking for it
JO   no, I don't remember that
BEA   how strange
JO   perhaps I wasn't there
BEA   oh yes, I'm sure you were
it was summer
the veranda doors were open
we were at the table
and you were sitting on my left
he didn't like spinach
so he was in a bad mood
and in order to praise mother's qualities
I brought up that whistling

ANNA   complete mistake
    that made him even more ratty
JO   I'm amazed you remember
BEA   I'll never forget it
JO   I mean what we were eating
ANNA   Bea's got a photographic memory for food
BEA   my father was mad about cucumbers
    on holiday
    always three weeks
    always France
    always the same campsite
    we always had to take
    twenty-one yellow cucumbers with us
    because he didn't like the green ones
ANNA   twenty-one yellow cucumbers
    and on top of that camping
    the whole family in one tent
    it makes me hyperventilate just to think about it
    standing in the queue for showers
    staring at the rows of flip-flops
    globs of soap everywhere from other dirty slobs
    slippery slimy floors
    and those communal lavatories
    stinking steaming holes
    in the hard ground
    when there's finally one free
    the paper's finished
    all that filth spattered up the walls
    stuck to the walls
    you'd have to wear waders up to your ears
    to survive it ... camping
JO   I do it for Rosie
    children love it
    they love tents
BEA   Adrian does it for the children too
JO   has Adrian got children?

ANNA and a wife lest we forget

BEA if you're trying to get at Jo
don't do it through me

ANNA I'm not trying to get at Jo
Jo's alright
apart from her thighs

JO *(ignores Anna, addresses Bea)* why do you always
go in for married men?

BEA more peaceful
plenty of time to yourself

ANNA and your career *(To Jo)*
how's your career doing?

JO good, very good
I've just been shooting a commercial today

BEA for what?

JO face cream with rejuvenating properties
a very good cream
I use it myself

ANNA one of those little spots
starring a young adolescent
a baby with skin like a peach
ow old are those models
on average?

JO sixteen, fifteen, fourteen

ANNA why don't you use someone of your own age?
someone who really needs rejuvenating cream

JO that's impossible
the camera sees everything

ANNA and it's not supposed to

JO it *is* supposed to
you have to have someone who
looks young and attractive
otherwise the product won't sell

BEA why should I have to look young and attractive
at my age?
why aren't I allowed to grow old with impunity

any more?
beautifully old with fine wrinkles
and juicy rolls of fat
why don't I live in a country
where men think that's sexy?

ANNA then emigrate to a third world country
Zimbabwe or somewhere
you'd go down well there
in our culture
a slim young appearance
excites a man more
than a large personality

JO Vincent thinks both are important

ANNA well Vincent's in luck then

BEA yes, you've got both Jo
you're perfect
you look good
you've got a terrific job
terrific legs
a man who loves you
a nice kid
you're slim, happy
what more do you want?

ANNA what everyone wants nowadays
muscular pecs
lip implants
the permanent pout
firm silicone breasts
as if you'd just stepped out of your own commercial

BEA would it still be a good fuck?
with all those tupperware attachments

ANNA it can only be second-rate
he can't feel it and she feels nothing

BEA I read in a woman's mag
that Jackie Onassis
had herself lifted for ten years

by Michael Jackson's plastic surgeon

JO   when Michael Jackson goes into town
he has himself made up
as an old black man
otherwise he gets ripped to shreds by fans
his make-up man has to go with him
to retouch him every so often

BEA   how do you know that?

JO   from a colleague in Hollywood

ANNA   they can rip Michael Jackson to shreds
for all I care
weirdo creep

BEA   he's a nice little mover though
(Bea does an impersonation)

ANNA   and Jackie Onassis was always a barbie
even when she was with Ken...nedy

JO   Elizabeth Taylor has had herself made
twenty years younger
she looks just as great as she used to

BEA   and she's got a boyfriend of twenty-six
who's madly in love with her

ANNA   but when she opens her mouth
it's just like a ventriloquist's dummy
or Lady Penelope from the Thunderbirds

BEA   Madonna's had her breasts and lips
enlarged
and Cher's had herself completely rebuilt

ANNA   I don't understand it
why healthy people let themselves be
chopped about of their own free will.
when animals or sportsmen are injected with rubbish
there's a public outcry, but no-one bats an eyelid
when women get themselves injected
with collagen,
have face lifts
get their fat lipo-suctioned

have their noses changed
have cheek-bones and ribs sawn out
look at American films
television series
the female newsreaders on CNN
all the women over the age of thirty-five
look the same
a string of young wrinkle-free sausages
with sad, deep-set eyes

BEA you can't have your eyes lifted
they've seen too much
old women are disgusting

JO *(to Anna)* I don't see what's
so terrible about it
it's a sign of the times
just be glad
that we have the opportunity
it's all part of our progress
the cosmetic industry
can do wonders nowadays
see it as an achievement
you want to look attractive too
don't you
and you Bea
you do too
you do it for yourself
you feel better
without dimples, wrinkles, stretch marks
and sagging skin
if you look good
it makes you feel a lot better
your life's so much fuller

ANNA and who decides whether you look good or not?

JO the mirror, the bathroom scales and I decide that
we decide that ourselves
if the mirror says lose two pounds
and the scales confirm it

then off come two pounds
give me another glass of wine Bea
(Bea pours. Anna takes glass.)

ANNA   start tomorrow or better still, start now
get as slim as a top model
lose two pounds a day
modern, career-minded women
point the way to success, beauty and slenderness
discover the delicious luxury
of a wine diet
the elegant way of losing weight
a sacrifice to give up food?
when you can drink two glasses
of sensual wine a day?
wine
a natural relaxant
which relieves tension and anxiety
tension and anxiety
which can be the cause of over-eating
wine
has the unique ability
to bestow a sense of contentment and well-being
wine
makes you feel
like the most wealthy, luxurious
pampered and irresistible woman
in the world
give yourself to wine
just as wine gives itself to you
and become the slender woman
of your dreams
(She raises her glass) cheers! to mother!

BEA   to mother!
JO   to mother!
BEA   last night I dreamed
that I was eating a blancmange
in a bath

which was filled to the top
with cream
and which was being licked empty
by ten men

ANNA   all married

JO   god how erotic
if only we'd been in it together
what were they wearing?

BEA   starkers all ten
down on all fours
licking away

JO   and then -

BEA   I got cold
then I woke up

ANNA   that was round about six
I heard you scrabbling about
in the kitchen
and after that
you stood under the shower for ages

BEA   that's right
I was still feeling rather sticky

ANNA   how are things with the old score board?

BEA   good
could be better
it'll do

ANNA   how often?

BEA   a day

ANNA   for instance

BEA   at the moment about three, four times

JO   a day?

ANNA   one day a week?

BEA   and in between a couple more times

JO   in between what?

BEA   office hours
Adrian often drops by in the lunch hour

ANNA   a lunch hour quickie?

JO   where do you do it then?
BEA   in the office
ANNA   what if someone comes in?
BEA   I just lock the door for a quarter of an hour
    I couldn't give a fuck
JO   on your desk?
BEA   or under it
JO   on the ground
BEA   on the hard floor
ANNA   no wonder
    you're always so shagged out
    oral as well?
JO   I'm not a great blow-fan
ANNA   blow-fan?
JO   if it goes on too long
    I get lockjaw
BEA   you're not doing it right
JO   how do you do it then?
BEA   (a) not with a full mouth in any case
ANNA   remote control
BEA   nothing else in your mouth
    no sweets or anything
    (She takes a bag of sweets out of her bag, throws it to Jo)
    here practice with these
    they're new
    Barrett's liquorice willies
    the longer you suck 'em
    the bigger they get
ANNA   and (b) Bea
BEA   (b) you should never swallow it
JO   is it supposed to be good or bad for the skin?
ANNA   too many calories
    people lived on it during the war
JO   instead of powdered egg
BEA   *with* powdered egg
    an aphrodisiac for the epicure

ANNA and you Jo
how's your score board doing?
when you can prise your thighs apart

JO sometimes you feel like it
sometimes you don't,
sometimes not for ages
I don't know
sometimes not for a whole month

BEA not for a whole month?

JO and then all of a sudden we do it again
and then we say to each other
god it's nice, isn't it?
why don't we do it more often?

ANNA the national average is two and a half times a week

JO it might well be
but sometimes
I just can't keep my mind on the job

BEA that'll be that half time then

JO I don't like doing things by halves
wham bam, thank you ma'am!
when I'm filming
I do it one hundred per cent
I don't want to be bothered by sex then

ANNA eyes front and nose to the grindstone

BEA not even to help you relax
it always bucks me up
what about Vincent
doesn't he want to do it more often?
men want to do it continuously don't they?
they have to satisfy their lust
otherwise they'll go looking for it elsewhere

ANNA are you sure he's not putting it about?

JO forget it but if he is
he won't be putting it in me any more

BEA but what's he supposed to do with his lib' then?

JO his lib'?

ANNA   lib' ... libido

JO   li-bi-do *(makes do-re-me hand movements, ends in fist.)*
     I've never found my g-string either

BEA   G-spot

ANNA   and Vincent is so musical

JO   in a completely different field

BEA *(to Jo)* shall we dance?
     (They dance and raise their glasses) to mother!

JO   to mother!

ANNA   shall we go?

BEA   not yet
     let's wait a bit

ANNA   what for?

BEA   for a photo
     I want to show you both a photo. *(Gets photo.)*
     everyone's in it
     look
     Anna is playing chess with her father
     and we're sitting in the garden with mother

ANNA   happy families

JO   it still was then

BEA   what on earth are we eating?
     oh yes custard tarts
     they weren't very nice
      the custard was all lumpy

JO   mother with that Chinese hat
     god I was thin then
     boyishly thin
     I thought I was Anna for a moment

BEA   you had gorgeous puppy fat when you were an adolescent

JO   but I didn't have those hips
     you could wear a thin gold chain round
     that was very in then
     a thin gold chain round your hips
     Sophia Loren had that
     beautiful shapely hips and a very narrow waist

you could ride around on those hips
those flanks
the most beautiful woman in the world

ANNA   except she was too fat
Marilyn Monroe would be too fat nowadays as well
she topped herself just in time

JO   die young stay pretty *(To Anna)*
that was always your motto

ANNA   so, your thighs chafe together do they?
does your husband make you diet?

JO   what do you mean?

ANNA   well you're so careful with what you eat
and he's a fitness fanatic isn't he?

JO   Vincent doesn't make me do anything
he accepts me as I am
if I'm a bit overweight
I go on a diet
he joins in as well
he wants to keep his figure too
small wonder with a mother like that
that woman is such a barrel of lard
she can never throw anything away
you don't throw food away
if you've been through the war
she's always snitching leftovers off plates
in the kitchen
Vincent hates her
I don't want to end up like that
and he wouldn't like it either
if I turned into a fat lump like her
Vincent is proud of me when I look good
he finds me more attractive when I'm slim
logical
your clothes hang better then

BEA   but a bit of fat's nice in bed isn't it?

ANNA   they hardly do it anyway

JO   I bet you don't remember the pencil test
I bet you don't remember us doing it
you had to put a pencil
under your breasts
and if the pencil or the pen
you could use a pen as well
stayed in place
you had to wear a bra
and the fashion was no bra
and a thin gold chain round your waist
when the pencil stayed in place
we started shoving all sorts of things under
a ruler, slices of bread, a lemon squeezer
and under yours a transistor radio - stereo
it all stayed in place

ANNA   you insisted on wearing a bra
it made you feel safe

JO   I wouldn't have dreamt of not wearing one
I thought it looked sloppy
and it was so constraining
those flobbering things
that you had to hump around with you
wherever you went like unwieldy ballast
my girlfriends used to say
are you still wearing a bra?
take that thing off
and I used to think
I must be square
I want to keep it on
the first bra I tried on
belonged to auntie Jean
who was staying the night with us
her bra was lying in the bathroom
an enormous thing
I put it on
shaking like a leaf

petrified
in case someone came in
much too big
I stuffed it full
of toilet paper
put on a tight sweater
a short skirt
and looked in the mirror
dead spit Sophia Loren
dead spit

ANNA   and now you're on the rejuvenating cream

BEA *(looks at the photo)* terrible eh
I've always loathed my body
and now I see myself in the photo
I think
what a pity
I was so beautiful then

ANNA   they used to do the pencil test in South Africa as well
a government official would stick a pencil in your hair
and then you had to shake your head
and if the pencil stayed in place
you'd be declared black
(They do the test: with Jo and Anna the pencil stays in place, with Bea it falls out)

BEA   that's clear then
same father
both black

ANNA   let's go

JO   hang on
I've got something else for you
(She takes two envelopes out of her bag, hands them to Bea and Anna. They open the envelopes, there's two twenty pound notes in each envelope)

ANNA   don't forget to thank him for the nice letter
I don't want the money
you can keep it

BEA   Anna don't be so childish
take it
you need it
ANNA   projection Bea
you're projecting
you need it
I don't need anything from that man
nothing
JO   that man just happens to be your father
ANNA   just happens to be yeh you're right
that man is not my father
and he never has been
he's never done anything
anything to remotely suggest he is
oh yes, he's chucked his money around
but I won't be bribed
he's a lost cause
I'm not interested in him
and he's not interested in me
JO   he reads all your articles
ANNA   can't say I've noticed
JO   he thinks they're good
ANNA   he can shove them up his backside
look you two can go out to eat
he's managed it again
even at a distance
he can manage to ruin my appetite
BEA   Anna come with us please
we're not here for him.
we're here for mother *(She tries to comfort her)*
ANNA   don't touch me
BEA   do it for mother.
do it for her
ANNA   don't be so ridiculous
mother is dead Bea
she's been dead eight years

and what does *he* do
on the anniversary of her death?
he manages to give Jo an empty envelope
an empty envelope
with forty quid in it

JO   at least he tried

ANNA   exactly
you're right
he tried
he had a go
he's been doing that his whole life
having a go
he had a go at mother
nice little single woman
with a nice little daughter
he had a go at the little daughter

BEA   shut up

ANNA   he made two more little children
or at least, he had a go
two flops
no boys more's the pity
no boys
oh well, Jo has succeeded at least
Jo's a career woman
Jo's got a good job
a nice husband
a marvellous son-in-law
an adorable child
Jo visits him
at least once a fortnight
Jo doesn't have a problem with it
Jo pretends that everything is fine
that nothing ever happened

JO   you're pushing me too far
I've controlled myself
you're mad or are you just jealous?

you've been getting at me
from the moment I walked in
just because I still see him
he's only human after all
and then you get at me
because I'm on a diet
just a couple of days on a diet
because you're scared
scared for yourself
because you haven't got the guts
because you're scared
to break through
because you're always on a diet
always have been
you don't even dare
to lick a stamp
in case it contains calories
you only ate baby food
weighed on a letter-scale
and even that you fed
to the cat
you deceived us
to our faces
you ruined our family life
with your tyrannisation
with your hunger strikes
all those scenes and arguments
just to get you to eat
and in the meantime
you were brilliant
top of the class
ten out of ten
you were good at that
but getting one mouthful of food down your throat
that you couldn't manage
father always loved you the most

because you were a model student
you were his favourite daughter
until you got sick

ANNA   I wasn't …

JO   hang on
I'm not finished yet
because mother
always stuck up for you
she eats more than you think Jo
more than you or Bea
she lied mother
she lied

BEA   she lied to protect us
she lied
because she was frightened
of his tempers

JO   to protect us
because she was frightened?
because in the meantime Anna was sick Beatrice
you could count her ribs
she could hardly walk up the stairs
on those little matchstick legs
she could hardly cycle to school
she was racked with pain
every time she sat down on a chair
she was always complaining of headaches
fine down grew on her cheeks
and her hair fell out
her periods stopped
she looked like Bergen-Belsen
when is your sister going to die?
someone asked at school
when is your sister going to die?
in the hospital she even managed
to disconnect the tubes
why did you do that?

why?
you were such a sweet child
before you got sick
so sweet
your nose in a book the whole day

ANNA   sick
I wasn't sick
(Anna runs off, immediately runs back, furious)

ANNA   will someone kindly remove their skid-marks
I can't go

JO   germophobia
don't go then

ANNA   ah I thought it was you
haven't you heard of toilet brushes?

JO   I haven't been out of this room yet
but now I'm going
what am I doing here?
anyone would think I was here for fun

ANNA   go with god but not on our bog

BEA   you can't go
I don't want you to go
I'll clean the toilet bowl

JO   this is ridiculous
can't she do it herself?

ANNA   I can but I won't
jamais de ma vie

BEA   I'll do it
I don't mind

JO   what is this?
is sister bully at it again?
she's an adult
a big girl
a woman
who writes articles about sex
sex in Europe

but her sister has to look after her
easy eh?
boarding with your big sister
ratbag
well you needn't think
you can bark your orders at me

ANNA   woof, woof, woof

JO   look Bea
what a little doggie
our little sister
(to Anna) our little pit-bull terrier
you've sunk your teeth into your sister
just like you used to sink them
into your mother
spoilt brat
(to Bea) you're a good substitute Bea
you seem deranged
father was right
she drove mother mad
and now she's driving *you* mad
little tyrant
what a mad house this is!
you're still sick

ANNA   I wasn't sick
I've never been sick
and I'm still not sick
I got sick of your nagging
that nagging
that I had to put on weight
I couldn't eat
and I couldn't care less
it was nice to feel hungry
I enjoyed it
a new day
a new hunger
my senses were sharpened

I heard, saw and smelt better
than anyone else
existence from the neck up
that's what it was all about
the absolute perfection
I had almost proved
that I was superior
that I had triumphed over nature
my head could rule
my body
my kingdom
it was marvellous
to defy hunger and cold
marvellous
to always be thinking of food
and still
be able to resist it
the days were endless
but it was worth it
I got thinner and thinner
I didn't want to be slim
I wanted to be thin
skinny
I wanted to see bones
no flesh
everything that went into my stomach
had to come out again as fast as possible.
my stomach had to stay pure
not stretch, above all, not stretch
I felt like
Kafka's hunger artist
I stood in front of the mirror
and I can say now
I was a bag of bones
you found me disgusting
people stared at me in the swimming pool

and even in my sleep
I was hungry
but I stood in front of the mirror
holding in that
remaining bit
of belly
and at night
I ran laps
round and round the garden
losing weight
gave me substance

JO   it was just your bad luck
that you had large breasts

BEA   bad luck

ANNA   bad luck yes
those stockades had to go
you can get as thin
as a board
but those breasts stay put
they get thinner
but more flaccid too
they started to droop
they weren't bee-stings
like yours Bea
that's what I wanted

BEA   god, you wanted that

ANNA   of course I wanted that
he said
you're turning into a woman
you're getting titties
you're starting to look like your mother
that was the worst thing
he could have said to me
mother was a woman yes
a mother, a housekeeper
she looked after him

and us
she was kind
very kind
even though she felt miserable
so sad
she was so dependent
I didn't want to be dependent
like her
not that, never
he always used to say
you look like a walking skeleton
you'll do your mother in
if you carry on like this
if you don't eat
she works her fingers to the bone for you
ungrateful witch
I didn't want to do mother in
I didn't want to disappoint her
so I'd take a mouthful
and sit there gagging
and you'd sit there
looking at me so accusingly
everything was my fault
but I couldn't
I just couldn't get it down
I had the feeling
I was so bad

BEA　　feelings can't be good or bad
it *was* awful at meal-times
dreadful
one look at him
was enough to put you off eating for good
the way he used to look at her food

JO　　and mother never used to say anything
she just clammed up

BEA　　out of fear that he didn't like the food

that he'd throw it across the room
that muck
ANNA   or he'd stuff himself
and then he'd stuff himself unbelievably
three quarters of a chicken
and we'd get the wing
do you think I felt like eating
with him sitting there
with his mouth glistening with grease
stuffing down that chicken
I could hear the bones crunching
I could hear the bones of that creature
crunching
inside that greasing gob
and I thought
he's chewing a dead body
what a torture
to have to sit at table with that man
BEA   a vampire
JO   her first husband chomped
and called women little dogs
her second husband gnawed
because he's a dog himself
oh for godsake
BEA   a bloodhound
JO   bloody hell
you make him out to be some sort of animal
ANNA   he's worse than an animal
he's a person
BEA   a person
in the beginning
he was nice
to mother and me
he took mother out
he gave me presents
I looked up to him

but I was afraid of him as well
one day mother said
we're going to go and live with uncle
he's going to be your new father
you'll have your own room
and in a while
a little sister or brother
JO   that was me, the rabbit
ANNA   the rabbit
BEA   yes she said
if we go and live there
you have to call him daddy
I didn't want to call him daddy
but he insisted
he said
if you don't call me daddy
I won't treat you like a daughter
JO   you never called him daddy
BEA   never
when we went to live there
in that big creepy house
everything changed
he stopped taking mother out
and there were no more presents
fortunately he was almost never at home
and when he was there
he sat in his study
mother wasn't my mother any more
absent
a shadow of what she once was
ANNA   he strangled her mentally
very slowly
excruciatingly slowly
he tightened the rope around her neck
JO   she was there too
she could have left

ANNA   we were there too
do you think she wanted to leave us alone
with that monster
JO   she could have taken us with her
BEA   where to?
how would she have managed it
she'd had everything she was capable of
everything she wanted
knocked out of her by him
JO   you two act as though mother was a saint
ANNA   no, not a saint
a victim
JO   he is an intelligent lonely man
he knows so much
ANNA   better
he knows everything better
JO   everyone respects him
BEA   he commands it
ANNA   he won't tolerate dissent
his opinion is the only one that counts
BEA   he despised her
he always insinuated that she was stupid
JO   never
not any more
he says that she was a good mother
ANNA   he always has to prove himself
every second of the day
he is always head of the table
even if it's a round one
JO   but actually
he's pathetic
a poor wretch who craves a bit of
love and attention
ANNA   a pain in the neck
a despot

a monomaniacal madman
a nutcase
a sex-murderer
the incarnation of the devil

JO   you blame him
for your own inability
to love someone
(Anna and Bea are seized by an uncontrollable laughing fit)
(Jo walks away)

BEA   blame
the sixty four thousand dollar question
the chicken, the egg or sour grapes
do you love him
that bungler, that blighter
(Jo says nothing)
why?
(Jo does not answer)
why?

JO   he's my father

BEA   does he love you then?

JO   of course
(Silence)
that's not important

BEA   why are you here?

JO   you know perfectly well why

BEA   I want to hear it from you

ANNA   what does it matter?
we're here aren't we?
we're here every year

JO   and now I'm going

ANNA   go then

BEA   yes go then
love to Vincent
and a kiss for Rose
(Jo exits, enters again. To Anna)

JO   from you too, Anna?

ANNA   from me too

(Jo exits)

ANNA   did you see those thighs Bea?

BEA   sure did

hard to miss

(Silence)

weren't you ever frightened of dying?

ANNA   I never thought I might die

never

it didn't matter what they said to me

it was all meaningless

death meant absolutely nothing

they might as well

have been speaking Russian to me

unimportant

totally unimportant

careful, malnutrition, death

it meant nothing

it's like having a strange fever

you're in a fever

and when you're in it

nothing at all matters

BEA   I've eaten him up

ANNA   who?

father

BEA   Adrian

I've just eaten him up

just like that

at night I lie in bed

with my warm friend

and all I can think of

is the fridge

or I'm sitting on the sofa

and he's sitting next to me

Adrian

and I feel my skin crawling
that man bores me so much
I can't do anything but - (eat)
or he's sitting on the sofa
and I come in
he doesn't look at me
he only looks at
my hands
to see what I'm holding
my little snack
doing something
with a tasty little snack
that's nice isn't it
a person's got to - (eat)
one thing
you can be certain of in life
otherwise you'll die
I've struggled my way through everything
the yellow brick road
mother goose
the muffinman
playboy
I've stuffed myself silly
like a child
who masturbates in secret
and who won't
escape punishment
our stomach is a juggler
our skin always yields
I know how to dress myself
I've got all sizes hanging in the wardrobe
8, 10, 12, 14, 16
because all weighing machines are liars
my doctor looks like
Twiggy's little sister
she says I just have to stop

I have stolen food out of
all my friends' fridges
I've knocked back the whole universe
I've got so much in me
I've had a bellyful
my cup runneth over
I'm sick of Adrian

ANNA   thrown up
ex-laxed
exit Adrian
you consume men
just like you bolt food
bite swallow gone

BEA   you knew didn't you?

ANNA   I'm your sister Bea

BEA   step-sister
it's in my genes
I'm sure it is
it's in my genes

ANNA *(sings for Bea)*
I'm a slice of my own pork pie
I'm a chop in need of grilling
if I don't eat
I feel devoid
a cannelloni without a filling
(Anna takes the forty pounds out of the envelope, gives it to Bea.)
here buy yourself something scrummy
my little butter pat

BEA *(raises her glass)* to mother!
there are so many things I'd like to have asked her

ANNA   me too
I always wonder
who would come to my funeral

BEA   and how many

ANNA   I'm sick with hunger
  cheers!
BEA   to mother!
ANNA   to mother!

Matin van Veldhuizen

Writer and director, began by doing the catering for a travelling
theatre company before taking up acting. She has performed and
directed with various theatre companies in the Netherlands. In 1978
she started to write for the theatre, both original plays and adaptations
of novels. She has also written children's stories and film scripts.
Since 1992 she has been artistic director of the Amsterdam theatre
company Theatergroep Carrousel, writing, producing and directing
plays.

Her obsession with food began early and is the inspiration for her play
Eat.

*'The pathological relationship that women have with food has been
bled dry by the media, but it's rare to see it on the stage. So the
subject approaches the realms of sociodrama, although the writer of
this light comedy has thankfully avoided social references. There's
plenty to recognise here, especially for women.'*

                                        Volkskrant 1991.

DOSSIER: RONALD AKKERMAN

Suzanne van Lohuizen
translated by Saskia A. Bosch
with special thanks to John Retallack

originally commissioned for the Theatre Company Frappant
by the René Klein Foundation.

*for Geert and Bart and Rob and Ivo and
Willem-Hendrik and René and all the others.*

Dutch premiere: 23rd of May, 1994
Director: Robbert Baars

CHARACTERS:

HE a patient
SHE a nurse

1.

SHE You are alone in your room. Your own room.
You have just returned from the funeral. You feel like dancing and
screaming and singing, out of sheer relief. You don't do it.
HE Because you are too decent for that.
SHE Because you know instead of singing you'll be howling
like a dog.
You hang up your coat.
You put the coffee in the filter and let the water drip through.
You put on some music just to break the silence.

You take his file from your bag.

HE   In the bag you find a packet of Gauloises, which you can't remember having put there.

SHE   You write down: On the 6th of May 1994, Ronald Akkerman, 34 years old, died of AIDS. His death was instantan - eous after an injection of 10cc Fentanyl, which was administered following repeated requests by the patient whilst he was fully conscious.

HE   Calm strong letters. Good handwriting.

SHE   You feel as though you might suffocate.

HE   And then, very quietly, the door opens.

SHE   You don't expect anyone.

HE   You don't have a guest.

SHE   You don't have a cat.

HE   You don't have a boyfriend.

SHE   You did have one. But he gave the keys back when he left.

HE   And then he comes in. In his dressing gown.
     A little absent-minded. A little preoccupied.

2.

SHE   Ronald? Your blood runs cold. Ronald?

HE   Hey, Nightingale.

SHE   He always called me Nightingale. I hated that.
     So it's you.

HE   I suppose so

SHE   What are you doing here?

HE   I'm looking for my cigarettes. I left them on the bedside table. I thought: Wouldn't it just be like Nightingale to take them with her.

SHE   I can't remember

HE   Gauloises. Look, there they are. Never tell lies, Nightingale.

SHE   My name is Judith.

HE   Have you got a light?

SHE   You want him to leave.

HE   In the kitchen?

SHE   You're afraid.

HE   Nice flat.

SHE   You think you're going mad.

HE   You don't mind if I smoke, do you?

SHE   You can smoke yourself to death if you like.

HE   Don't get bitchy, Nightingale. I liked the funeral.
Didn't you? Everyone was there. Even Dad. Stubborn old fool
that he is. He didn't look well. Tired. Aged. Must be quite
something, burying your own son. To see him standing there,
amongst all those queens. What a laugh.

SHE   Could you please stop that.

HE   You turn away because you don't want to face him.

SHE   You can hear your heart beating in your chest.

HE   He's just standing there.

3.

SHE   What do you want?

HE   Aren't you glad to see me?

SHE   Honestly, no.

HE   Fine, Nightingale. Honesty above all. Never mind. Always
tell the truth, if only for truth's sake. I am. I am happy to see you.
Did anyone ever tell you you're pretty? You are much prettier
than I thought.

SHE   Very flattering. You never even looked at me.

HE   I was almost blind, remember?

SHE   You sit down at the table. You take a deep breath. Calm
down, Judith. Everything is alright. You've had a hard time.
Perhaps it's all been a bit too much for you. Everything is alright.

HE   You glance through the file. That helps.

SHE   23rd of March 1993. Team meeting. District C has
received an application of an AIDS patient with CMV retinitis.
Eye-infection. Treated in hospital. Port-a-Cath was inserted.
Requires twice daily assistance with administering the IV
infusion. Otherwise no help needed. But not out of the question:

Yes, most probably further nursing care required in the near future or thereafter.

HE   You see. To me you were a shadow, shuffling through my room. A shadow in an apron. How was I supposed to know you had so many freckles?

SHE   Don't touch me!

HE   Don't worry. Hallucinations aren't contagious.

SHE   Go. Please go. Now.

HE   I've only just arrived. How about some coffee?

SHE   He takes the cups.

HE   Milk and sugar?

SHE   He pours the coffee.
You look at him thinking: I've never seen him doing that.
Because when you first came to him, he couldn't do that anymore.
And you know, suddenly you realise that he's really there.
He'll always be. He has become a part of you.

HE   Which is exactly what you've been trying to avoid.
At all costs. Sugar and milk?

SHE   Yes.

HE   Careful. It's hot.

SHE   You take the cup from him. You hold it with both hands. As long as you can bear it. Then you drop it. It shatters on the floor.

HE   Nightingale! That's not like you at all.

4.

SHE   He walks through the room as though he's always been there.

HE   Yes. Nice flat. Pretty. Colourful curtains. A vase with flowers. Everything taken care of. In order. Just as I thought. No doubt, Nightingale has got it all planned out. She knows how to make things work. She won't get AIDS. She is far too decent for that. Right? Isn't AIDS only for bad people?

SHE   He takes the funeral card from the mantelpiece.

HE   Ronald Akkerman has given up his fight against AIDS on the 6th of May 1994. We are all very sad.
You too, Nightingale. Just admit it. You too.

SHE   You look at your red hands.

HE   You're crying. Hey, Nightingale, you're crying.

SHE   Don't call me Nightingale!

HE   Funny. We've known each other so briefly.
Yet it seemed almost like a kind of marriage. Didn't it?

SHE   Depends on what you call a marriage.

HE   Not a good one, I'll admit. We were condemned to each other. I'm not that good with women, you know.

SHE   You gather the broken pieces of china. You say:
Yes, I know.

HE   But we were good at bickering. That also means something.

SHE   Why on earth did you come?

HE   Who can say?
To quarrel some more? For my so-called peace of mind?

SHE   Does anybody ever care about my peace of mind?
You died. I looked after you and dammit - you died.

HE   Don't swear, Nightingale.

SHE   I'll swear if I want to.

5.

HE   Why did you do it?

SHE   Do what?

HE   Look after me.

SHE   That's my job.

HE   Now that's what I find so brilliant about you.
Your professionalism. This unbearably brilliant professionalism of yours.

SHE   You were in my district, that's all.

HE   Just my luck.

SHE   Nobody wanted to do it. Everybody was afraid.

HE   Not you.

SHE   Me too. Dick was furious. He wanted me to refuse.

He didn't want me to go. We had plans. We were going to get
married. We wanted a child.
Suddenly he wanted to wait. He said it was too risky.
I thought that was ridiculous.
He didn't want me to tell his family. Or his friends.
He said he'd forbid me to go.
I said: It isn't up to you to forbid me to do anything.

6.

HE   The first time you came in.
Hair in a bun. That pin, that had to hold everything in place.
Didn't it hurt? Your hair stretched the skin on your head.
And that smile.
That 'you-won't-find-out-anything-about-me' smile.
That 'nothing-is-wrong-with-me. I-find-this-quite-normal.
I-find-AIDS-quite-normal. I-find-gays-quite-normal.
I-don't-know-them. But-I-find-them-quite-normal.'
That smile.

SHE   I was nervous. Is that so strange?

HE   I thought that was strange, yes.

SHE   And?

HE   You should have seen yourself. The first thing you did.

SHE   I made tea.

HE   You put rubber gloves on. And an apron.
A surgical mask for your mouth. You looked like a Martian.
And then, yes then you made tea.

SHE   Those were the instructions.

HE   You can smell fear, you know. Dogs can smell it.
I smelt it too. I hated you. Right from the start.

SHE   Is that what you came to tell me? You can save yourself the
trouble. I already knew. Have you finished?

HE   Not yet.

SHE   I have.

7.

SHE   You turn round and walk to the kitchen.
You throw the pieces of the coffee cup in the bin.
You take a sponge. He is standing at the sink.

HE   And you hated me. Right, Nightingale?

SHE   What I hated most was your damned arrogance.

HE   Of course. Those who die should know their place.

SHE   You return to the room.
There he is, sitting in one of your comfortable chairs.
His feet on the small glass table. The table, the file, everything is
smothered with coffee. You take the file and wipe it with the
sponge.

HE   It'll be a terrible mess.

SHE   Mind your own business.
You spread the damp pages on the floor to dry.

HE   Sorry.

SHE   He lights a cigarette.

HE   You were the first nurse who came. You were the beginning
of the end.

SHE   Was it my fault that you became ill?

HE   Was it mine?

SHE   You don't answer. You scrub the table which only gets
dirtier.

HE   Answer me, Nightingale. It was my fault, wasn't it?
Normal people don't get AIDS.
Normal, respectable, careful people don't have to screw around.
And if they just can't help it, they'd use condoms. Wouldn't they?
Homosexuals are simply unnatural.
Too much sex is unnatural anyway.
And unhealthy.
That just shows you.
I've only got myself to blame. Right?

SHE   I never said any of that.

HE   But that's what you thought. It was all in your mind.
Just admit it, Nightingale.

SHE   You don't say anything.

HE   You don't say anything.

SHE   What the hell do you want me to say?

8.

HE   It's now three years ago since Leo died. One and a half
years before I got ill. Of course we often asked ourselves whether
I was infected too. I just didn't want to know it.
I had to have the strength for the two of us to go on.
Sometimes I almost wished that I'd get ill too. Then I didn't want
to be careful anymore at all. I wanted to go with him. I wanted to
feel what he felt. I wanted to be like him.
Two months after his death I decided to have the test.

SHE   You don't want to listen, but you listen. You watch him
while he gets up and walks to the window.
The way he stares outside.

HE   When I got the result I went to sit on a bench in the park.
I looked at the ducks. The rays of the sun were glittering on the
water. My mind was empty. Completely empty. I just sat there.
A little girl kept racing past on her bike. She fell. She'd grazed
her knees on the gravel. She cried hysterically. I just watched her.
I could have tried to console her. I didn't do anything.

SHE   The way he turns round.
The way the ash drops from his cigarette.

HE   Do you know what I mean? Life has become a film.
You don't take part in it. I was a spectator. And I tried to keep
that feeling as long as I could. It reassured me. I didn't feel
anything. That was nice. Oh God yes. That was nice.

SHE   The way his eyes search for an ashtray.
The way he stubs the end of his cigarette in the empty coffee cup.

HE   Of course I couldn't keep that up.
I became furious. Furious and desperate.
My life wasn't meant to be like this, you see. If I ever thought for
one moment that I wanted to die too, then I was now convinced
that I didn't. My God. Never have I felt so betrayed.

SHE   The way he sits down again.

HE   I became streetwise. I wanted the seedy side of life. The abyss. I wanted to challenge the world. I made love on every street corner. I used to be attractive you know. Wherever I opened my flies, men went down on their knees. When it was over I'd turn and walk away without looking back.

SHE   I don't see the point of all this.

HE   Do I shock you? Oh, Nightingale. Didn't it ever occur to you that not all people share your standards of respectability?

SHE   It never crossed your mind that someone else might be at risk?

HE   You're still a bitch, that's what you are. So that is the only thing you can think of. How poisonous I was. How contagious. Don't worry. I knew that very well myself.
I always stuck to the rules. I wasn't that sick.
But I did want something else you know.
I wanted to live. Funny isn't it?
I wanted to live life as long as that was still possible. I wanted to have my fair share.
And above all I didn't want to think about Leo.

SHE   And? Did it help?

HE   Sometimes it did, sometimes it didn't.
I had my job. Journalist. I worked harder than ever.

9.

HE   And then one day, you notice. That you can't see so well. That it seems you're going blind. It starts with one eye.
The image becomes blurred. Patchy.
At first it doesn't dawn on you. You think, perhaps I need glasses. You feel you can't focus very well. That there's a kind of mist over the lens.
Cytomegalovirus.
I hadn't expected it to start like that. I wasn't prepared. I didn't know I should have seen a doctor immediately. When I was admitted to hospital it was almost too late. But they treated it.

After about ten days I was allowed to go home.

SHE   I know. March 1993.

HE   You know what happened. But do you know what it means? When you can't read the paper anymore.
Can't write an article.
When you can't pick up your own glass.
Can't make your sandwiches.
When you trip over your own chair.
Did you have any idea about that when you came in with your bag full of stuff under your arm?

SHE   What do you think? You and your special illness.
That you're the only one?
People get ill you know. They get MS or a cerebral haemorrhage or a heart-attack. And then they need help.
Yes. You happened to be my first patient with AIDS.
Maybe I had no idea.
Maybe I didn't know how horrible it was.
Or how horrible it would become.
All that didn't give you the right to treat me like dirt.

HE   I didn't treat you like dirt.

SHE   You just pretended I didn't exist.

HE   I had enough people who wanted to help me. My neighbour did the shopping. My sisters cooked for me.
Lydia on Monday, Jeanette on Friday.
Once a week my mother would come to clean the house.
I had friends. Who really knew me.
To whom I didn't have to explain anything.
I didn't want strangers.
I still could do a great deal myself.
Only that damned daily infusion.

SHE   Half an hour a day.

HE   Two times half an hour.

SHE   Every time I came in everybody would go quiet.
Your mother was embarrassed because you didn't want to talk to me.

HE   Where could I start?

With Adam and Eve?
The Citizens Advice Bureau?
Jesus. Half the world suffers from AIDS and you had simply
decided that it was all my fault.

10.

SHE   You benefited from the treatment. The infection responded
to the medication.

HE   Yes. I didn't go completely blind, so I suppose I was lucky.
When I wasn't too tired I could almost lead a normal life. With
help from my colleagues and a dictating machine I even tried to
work again.
Unfortunately, I couldn't tolerate the AZT that I was given any
more. The dosage had to be reduced.
I started to get symptoms of paralysis
Pins and needles in my hands and feet.
One night when I wanted to go to the loo, I fell. My legs gave way.
I hardly made it back to my bed.
I was admitted for a blood transfusion. You arranged a whole load
of facilities. The hospital bed in the sitting-room. The crutches.
The commode. Folders full of instructions and advice.
You started talking about a wheelchair.

SHE   You felt insulted. Angry.

HE   When Leo died I promised myself one thing:
If it ever happens to me I won't go in a wheelchair.
Never. I'd rather die.

SHE   Jesus. I wanted to help you.

HE   Yes. That was your kick. You'd be the perfect nurse.
That was the star part you had chosen for yourself.
With me as supernumerary. You could handle this.
You knew how to live. And how I should die.
You had so many ideas. I'm sorry. I'm really sorry, that I didn't
fit into your concept of the world.

SHE   You were sitting in your bed like the Shah of Persia.
Remote control for the TV, for the video, for the CD-player.

You'd have liked a remote for the people around you. Your
sisters, your mother, your friends. You had everybody running
around for you.

HE   They were quite happy to do it.

SHE   There was always something.

Are my slippers under my bed?

Did Edwin call, or Peter?

Where is my razor?

I don't want those striped pyjamas.

I want the blue silk ones.

Isn't it time for my orange-juice?

Read me the paper. The death notices. Do I know anyone?

The science section. Is there anything in it about a new cure.

Top of the list was whether your cigarettes were on your bedside
table.

Never a 'thank you.' Or, 'how are you actually?'

Not surprising that none of them could stick it out.

HE   You did.

SHE   I did, yes.

HE   You had your responsibility. And your sense of duty. And
your high, high standards of professionalism.

SHE   Which you defied.

HE   But you refused to give up. Till that morning, when was it,
the beginning of September?

11.

HE   You'd been visiting for about three months. Every morning
at exactly nine o'clock.

The sound of the key in the lock. The door opens.

That cheerful professional smile in your voice.

How is it today, Ronald?

It's not good. It's bad, nurse. Bad. I'm going to die, you know.

Apart from that everything is fine.

You, icily professional:

Don't make it more difficult than it already is, Ronald.

How could you know, know what I knew.

That I'd been shitting myself in my bed.

That I'd been lying in my own muck for about three hours.

That I didn't have the strength to get up and wash my own arse.

That the only thing I could do was to keep you at a distance, growling like a scabby dog.

What did you know about shame, eh?

Bless human memory that nobody has to remember his mother changing his last dirty nappy.

Nobody. Except me.

It stinks in here you said. You opened a window.

Yes, it stinks in here. I'm lying here in my own filth till madam decides it's time to wash me.

You drew the blanket back. You pulled yourself together within a second.

The sound of your efficient pacing up and down.

I heard water running in a bucket.

I heard the door of the cupboard.

You took some bed linen.

Dammit hurry up.

You were looking for clean pyjamas.

Which ones do you want, the blue silk ones or the striped ones?

I don't give a damn. I don't give a fucking damn.

You put your gloves on.

SHE   You said: What a waste of your diplomas.

To be doing the job of a sewerman.

HE   For a moment everything was silent. No more efficient footsteps. No more rustling of the wrapping of the gloves. Then with a smack you put down the bucket and walked out of the room.

SHE   I took my coat.

HE   I screamed. Help me. Nurse, please help me.

I pleaded. I squirmed. I cried.

Snot was running from my nose.

SHE   I wanted to leave.

HE   But you came back.

You took the bucket and washed me.

Very carefully you turned me on one side.
You folded the dirty sheets. You laid out fresh ones.
You washed my legs, my back, my bottom.
The water was warm. Nice and warm.
You blew my nose. I smelled soap.
I wanted to cry. But I didn't.
You turned me on my other side.
Dirty sheets away, clean ones instead.
You washed me again.
I didn't think I'd ever be clean again.
But I was.

12.

SHE   He gets up and walks through the room.
He takes a small bottle from the chimney and takes the lid off.
HE   Nice perfume. Must be quite expensive?
SHE   He sprays a little into the room.
HE   You want to know something funny, Nightingale?
From that moment on I started to feel attached to you.
SHE   Well you never showed it.
HE   I looked forward to your visits. Those efficient footsteps.
That bitchy voice. Those hands that washed me.
The diarrhoea lasted for weeks. I became weaker every day.
I couldn't do anything myself anymore.
SHE   I thought you were going to die.
HE   They all thought I was going to die. Everybody started to
show up again. Did you ever notice that before?
Everybody scrambles for the last breath.
I wasn't left alone for a moment.
Day and night I had someone at my bedside.
And they all wanted to talk about saying goodbye and accepting
and dying peacefully. I didn't want to die peacefully.
I didn't want to die at all.
And the last thing I wanted was to talk about it.
You never talked to me. At that time you came three times a day,

but you wouldn't talk.

How are you today Ronald? But I didn't even have to answer.
Whenever I did you wouldn't listen. For you it was all quite
simple. Diagnosis AIDS and then it's just a question of shaking
pillows and washing buttocks.

SHE　　That's what you thought.

HE　　One time you washed my balls. I got a hard on.

I couldn't see whether you blushed. Did you blush?

SHE　　You're still standing there with the sponge in your hands.
You want to throw it right in his face.
You control yourself. You walk to the kitchen. At the door of the
kitchen you turn. You shout. Yes! Yes, I blushed!
If that's what you really want to know.
Piss off. Please, just piss off.
You rinse the sponge under the tap. You don't want to cry.
You wet your face with your hands. The cold water feels good.
You dry yourself with a tea-towel. You wait for a long time.
Till you're calm. Till you think he must have left by now.
You return to the room.

13.

SHE　　He hasn't left.
He is standing near the bookcase, turning the pages of a
photo album.

HE　　Everybody thought I was going to die, and you went on
holiday. Of course. You can't change all your plans for every
minor setback.

SHE　　Leave my stuff alone.

HE　　Autumn half-term 1993. With Dick in the Ardennes.
Five days bad weather. Had fun anyway. Long walks in the mist.

SHE　　Keep off I said.

HE　　Got lost in the pouring rain.
Walked for hours along a winding stream. Finally we crossed it.
Everything wet. Dick pours the water out of his wellies.

Is that Dick? Handsome guy. Nice body.

Clearly doesn't belong in the high-risk category.

SHE   You are disgusting.

HE   Although you can never be quite sure about these things.

Warming up by the fire.

Me in my sleeping bag on the sofa. Towel round my wet hair.

Dick is cooking sausages in the kitchenette.

Lots of lying in bed. Lots of making love?

SHE   Lots of reading.

HE   Looks cosy.

SHE   And lots of rowing.

HE   Rowing? Blimey, Nightingale.

SHE   Why did you say that. You didn't want to.

It's none of his business.

HE   Not so much fun after all?

SHE   The holidays were meant to bring us back together again.

Dick had organised it all. He expected a lot.

HE   But?

SHE   I didn't really want a holiday.

I wasn't in the mood for it.

When I looked at Dick, how strong he was, and how healthy,

then I thought that was - I don't know. Unfair.

HE   How nice of you. That you did think about me sometimes.

SHE   I didn't want to. I didn't want to think about you.

Dammit, could I help it that you were going to die?

But I kept seeing you, how you were lying there. The thought that

everything would be over when I returned.

That I had let you down.

The holiday was a disaster.

14.

HE   I looked forward to your coming back.

SHE   When I came back you weren't dead at all. You had

recovered. The bowel infection had improved and you were

recuperating fast.

HE   I had put on some weight.

I thought you might be pleased about that.

SHE   I don't know whether I was pleased.

Maybe, yes. I suppose so. But above all I was angry.

I was furious.

HE   I had ruined your holiday and now I refused to die.

SHE   Yes.

HE   Sorry.

SHE   He turns a few more pages in the photo album.

HE   Christmas at Dick's mother's.

All the brothers and sisters gathered by the Christmas tree. She likes to have her children around her.

SHE   It was my last Christmas with Dick.

HE   It was my last Christmas.

SHE   I wasn't on call And I'd taken a few extra days off.

During that time you went to your sister.

HE   We behaved as though I wasn't ill at all.

Everybody did.

I was able to walk with a stick.

We went to midnight mass.

With my little cousin Freddy who was four years old.

Christmas in the bosom of my family.

Who would ever have thought.

Leo and I used to go skiing. He hated all these family duties.

I thought it was fun. I hadn't expected it, but I really thought it was fun.

I had bought a candle for Freddy.

A snowman candle. He was pleased with it.

He was allowed to burn it during the Christmas dinner.

Slowly the snowman collapsed. First the hat. Then the eyes.

They melted away and trickled down.

Look, said Freddy. The snowman is crying, because he's going to die. Do you cry too, uncle Ronald? Because you are going to die?

I took him on my lap. I said: Yes, I do. Sometimes I do cry about that.

Me too, he said.

Then he quickly blew out the flame. And then we all laughed.

15.

SHE   You don't know what to say.

He turns the page.

HE   There aren't many left.

Dick drinking champagne on New Years Eve.

Dick on the ice wearing the new jumper I knitted for him.

Dick squatting down for the first crocuses.

That's the end. No more.

Empty pages.

SHE   We broke up in spring.

HE   You never told me.

SHE   Did we ever tell each other anything?

HE   Of course not.

Any decent nurse keeps her private life strictly separate from her work.

SHE   You were in hospital. You had meningitis. The doctors thought you wouldn't make it.

I - I didn't want to let you down. Not this time.

I wanted to visit you.

Dick thought that was absurd.

HE   Unprofessional.

SHE   Another row.

He just didn't understand.

And I didn't feel like explaining it all over again.

It had become quite clear to me how different we were.

He left the key on the table and slammed the door behind him.

HE   Poor Nightingale.

SHE   You don't have to feel sorry for me.

The papers of the file have dried.

You gather them and leave them in a pile.

A lumpy pile, full of brown stains.

HE   I mean it. You must have been lonely.

SHE   I was.

You just flick through the pages.

HE   It was my third admission into hospital. And again I didn't die. You must admit, they didn't get rid of me that easily.

SHE   When you recovered this time I was happy for you. Really happy.

HE   I went home again.

SHE   The first time I visited you, you asked me to order a wheelchair.

HE   You see. Man is fickle.

SHE   You were happy with it. You were proud of it. You wanted me to take you out in it.

HE   I knew it would be my last spring.

SHE   We went to the park. I put you in a spot sheltered from the wind. In the sun.

HE   I saw colours. Vague blotches. A mass of yellow.

SHE   Daffodils. I picked them for you.

HE   Suddenly I burst out crying.

SHE   I tried to calm you down.

HE   But you were crying too.

SHE   You throw the file on the floor.

The piled up papers are spread out again.

You sit down at the table. Your head in your hands.

You want him to go.

But you know that it's too late now.

That you'll have to go through to the end.

16.

HE   Nightingale, what was the worst thing?

SHE   The worst thing was, that I started to love you.

HE   Yes. That was stupid of you.

SHE   You were so cheerful. You made all sorts of plans. You still hoped to go on a long trip. To India, that was your greatest wish.

HE   And then you'd come with me. To carry all the medical
  supplies.

SHE   On Saturdays you'd look up the property section in the
  paper. You wanted to move.
  You wanted a big house in the country. A villa.

HE   If I was going to die anyway then I wanted to die like a king.

SHE   You never talked about dying. You were - you were full of
  life. I admired you.

HE   You were jealous of me.

SHE   It seemed - as if suddenly you knew how to live.
  Better than us. Better than me.

HE   Gosh. You almost wished you had AIDS yourself.

SHE   Sorry.

HE   Never mind.

SHE   You seemed happy.
  I was wondering whether you knew how ill you were.

HE   Of course I knew.

SHE   Day and night you needed help. At night a nurse, during the
  day someone from the home care service.
  Your family came often. You were nice to them.
  You were nice to everyone, except to me.

HE   Somebody had to take the hardest blows.
  You had the broadest shoulders.

SHE   Of course. I had my professionalism.

HE   Which I found so brilliant.

SHE   Very flattering.

HE   Of course I was nice to everybody. They were distressed.
  They shed tears at my bedside. I had to make it easy for them.
  No?
  You have to be a kind of nice sick person.
  You didn't cry.
  You made it easy for me.
  You arranged and you organised.
  Strict schedules. Rules to be kept.
  The ones who were too loud or stayed too long were chucked out.

SHE   And then you'd be angry about it.
You argued about everything.

HE   I enjoyed arguing with you. It relieved me.
It gave me the feeling that I was somehow still in charge.
But in fact I was grateful to you.
I had no energy left for trouble with my family.
Or my friends. I wanted them to let go.

17.

HE   Once I had a sparrow. The cat had got him. The poor
creature was still alive, but it looked like it wouldn't hold out much
longer. It was lying very still on its back with its little legs in the
air.
And me, idiot, I wanted to save it. I took it in my hands.
It tried to escape.
I put it in a small box. The whole night it was squeaking and
fluttering. I tried to calm it down by holding it very carefully.
But that only made things worse.
The next morning I walked out of the room. Just for a moment.
When I came back two minutes later it was dead. Two minutes.
Just long enough to slip away.
Poor little thing.
You see?

18.

SHE   Give me a cigarette.

HE   You don't even smoke.

SHE   Dammit give me a cigarette.

HE   As you wish.

SHE   He gives you a cigarette.
He lights one himself. He coughs.
You can't imagine that the day will come when you won't hear
that coughing anymore.

HE   And I had a lot to arrange.
The funeral. Didn't you think it was a good idea,
to ask everybody to bring daffodils?
I did it for you.

SHE   Thanks a lot.

HE   I had to decide what would happen with my stuff.
Who'd get the CDs, the books, the paintings. I had many
paintings. Some of them were worth a lot of money.
When you haven't got any kids you have to think of everything.
My cousin Freddy got the globe with the little light.

SHE   He put the snowman on your grave.

HE   I wrote to my father. We hadn't seen each other for at least
six years.
Dad, I wrote, it's nearly over. Perhaps we can still shake hands
before it's too late?
He didn't reply. I knew he wouldn't. But all the same...

SHE   He phoned the office. The day before yesterday.

HE   When it wasn't necessary anymore. Strange man.
And I had to have several talks with the GP.
Filling in forms, signing a declaration. She wanted to help me,
but only according to the rules.
A second doctor came to visit me.
It reassured me to know that it was settled.

SHE   I don't want to listen to you anymore.

HE   You have to. You never listened to me. Now you have to.

SHE   I didn't know anything about it.

HE   Nobody knew anything about it.
Some things you just have to do on your own.
Death, Nightingale, is a man with flowers on his hat.
I had decided to make friends with him.

19.

SHE   You never had the chance to travel to India.

HE   I got pneumonia in April.

SHE You coughed day and night.

HE The GP wanted to admit me to hospital.

I asked her what my chances were. She didn't have much hope.

I decided to stay home.

SHE You didn't want to see anyone.

HE I didn't want to be that sparrow.

SHE Your mother phoned every day. She was desperate to visit you.

HE I couldn't stand her presence.

Everytime she came in I felt like whimpering. Like a little boy, trying not to cry when he's cut his knee.

Don't cry. Don't cry.

You succeeded. Until you got home and cracked up.

Then she had you exactly where she wanted you.

To rock you in her arms, to comfort you, to salve the wound and dry your tears.

Then you would have been saved.

But now it was too late for her to save me.

In the end, I only had you. And you didn't want to save me.

SHE Sometimes I would visit you four times a day.

My colleagues were worried. They thought it was all too much for me. They wanted me to delegate. I refused.

They thought I couldn't cope.

They insisted that at least the night duties should be taken over by someone else.

HE I preferred to have you. I'd become attached to you, didn't I tell you?

SHE I wanted it to be over. I longed for it.

God, how I longed for it.

HE You wanted to get rid of me.

SHE I couldn't bear it any longer.

That husky breathing. That silence after every breath.

And then still another one.

HE I felt as though I was going to suffocate.

And I knew that was exactly how it would happen.

SHE They gave you oxygen. You breathed.

20.

HE The morning of the 6th of May.

I'd had a rough night.

I'd hardly had any sleep.

I'd waited till you were there.

The nightnurse had gone home.

You gave me my medicine.

You walked out of the room to get the mail.

When you had left I called the GP.

SHE I came in. I said, there's a card for you from Scotland.
From someone called David. You smiled. I wanted to give it to
you. You didn't take it. You said-

HE Nightingale, I've had enough.

I don't want this anymore.

SHE You were whispering. I could hardly hear what you were
saying.

HE I called the GP. She'll come at half-past eleven.

SHE I understood immediately.

I went ice-cold.

You said -

HE I want you to stay with me.

SHE I didn't answer.

I put clean sheets on your bed. I washed you.

I arranged some fresh flowers and put David's card on your
bedside table.

I put the cigarettes in my bag. Without even realising.

I packed my apron, the glove-box, the syringes.

I sat with you and held your hand.

I listened to your breathing. Which stopped and started again.
Over and over.

Then the doorbell rang.

I opened the door for the doctor.

I went to your bed.

I kissed you on your forehead.

I said: I'm going now, Ronald.

You said: Bye Nightingale.
Then I left.

21.

HE   You went to the park.
SHE   I sat on a bench and thought:
        At this moment the doctor is sitting at his bedside.
        Very still. For a very long time.
        Now she asks Ronald if he is sure.
        Now Ronald nods.
        Now she picks up her equipment.
        Now she gives him the injection.
        Carefully she pulls the needle out of his arm.
        And now she waits until the breathing stops.
HE   It didn't take long.
SHE   I sat there for at least three hours.
HE   Then you went home.
SHE   I threw my bag in the hallway. I didn't touch it
        until today.
HE   You have asked for time off work.
SHE   I didn't want to see anyone. I didn't want patients.
        No colleagues who'd already said that I didn't keep enough
        distance. No friends.
        I was lying in bed. I never wanted to get up again.
        I didn't sleep. I didn't eat.
        All the time I saw you. And all the time I asked myself
        whether I should have stayed with you.
HE   You were at the funeral.
SHE   Yes.
HE   You feel as though you're a failure, don't you Nightingale?
        You'd be the perfect nurse. Florence Nightingale.
        But when it really mattered you let me down.
SHE   That's mean!
        You couldn't ask it of me. Not that.

I could never have done it.

If you'd ever asked yourself who I really was you'd know that.

HE   You wanted me dead. But you didn't want to do it.

You didn't want to get your hands dirty.

All of a sudden your gloves weren't sufficient anymore.

Yes, Nightingale, the infection is much filthier than you would expect. You can try to protect yourself.

Three litres of chlorine and a surgical mask will do.

But all the rest. What creeps under your skin.

Not even ten aprons will help you keep that out.

There is no antiseptic against life, Nightingale.

You'll get dirty anyway.

You are a participant. An accomplice.

I thought you were a coward. A coward and a hypocrite.

22.

SHE   You put your head in your hands. You cry in despair.

You say: I couldn't. I just couldn't do it.

He comes to you. Clumsily he strokes your hair.

HE   I know. And you know what? Dying is something you've got to do on your own.

Silly of me, to forget that for a moment.

Even that sparrow knew it.

Listen, I'm going now. Anyway thanks for everything.

Keep the cigarettes if you like. I don't like the taste anymore.

SHE   You look up.

You still want to say something. But suddenly he's disappeared.

You just sit there, in your empty room.

You stare at the coffee stains on the rug. The ash on the floor.

The papers from the file, scattered around.

You say out loud: Bye Ronald.

HE   Bye, Nightingale.

Suzanne van Lohuizen

She studied at the Conservatory of Dramatic Art in Arnhem. In 1977
she completed her training as a teacher of Dutch and shortly
afterwards began a career as an actress with a political theatre group
called Proloog. She also began writing and directing plays for adults
and children. In 1992 she was awarded the Dutch/Flemish Dramatic
prize for 2 children's plays:
Have you seen my little boy?
The house of my life.

She says of her work:

'*The struggle which sets the child against the world which surrounds
him, is a hard one. I don't write for children from a sense of
mission, but because I still feel very close to them emotionally.*'

OTHER TITLES BY AURORA METRO PRESS

MEDITERRANEAN PLAYS BY WOMEN
ed. Marion Baraitser

A collection of astonishing plays by women from countries geographically linked but politically divided.

Twelve Women in a Cell, (trans. Marion Baraitser / Cheryl Robson) a play written after a period of captivity in Egypt by dissident writer **Nawal el Saadawi.**

The End of the Dream Season, (trans. Helen Kaye) a woman doctor outwits her friends and relations to retain her inheritance, by Israeli writer **Miriam Kainy.**

Libration, (trans. Lola Lopez Ruiz) a mysterious intense and comic two-hander about two women who meet in a city park at night, by Catalan writer **Lluisa Cunillé.**

Mephisto, from the novel by Klaus Mann, (trans. Timberlake Wertenbaker) the story of a German actor who sells his soul to Nazi ideology by the eminent French writer/director **Ariane Mnouchkine.**

Harsh Angel, (trans. Rhea Frangofinou) a gentle Chekhovian tale of a family torn by the partition of their native land, written by Cypriot writer **Maria Avraamidou.**

Veronica Franco (trans. Sian Williams / Marion Baraitser) describes the life of a sixteenth century Venetian courtesan and poet, by Italy's foremost woman writer **Dacia Maraini.**

a great opportunity for those who don't see much live theatre by women to know what they've been missing. Everywoman Magazine

Price: £9.95   **ISBN 0-951-5877-3-0**

SIX PLAYS BY BLACK AND ASIAN WOMEN WRITERS
ed. Kadija George

A landmark collection of plays for stage, screen and radio demonstrating the range and vitality of Black and Asian writing.

My Sister-Wife by **Meera Syal**, a taut thriller about two women who discover they are both married to the same man.
'A phenomenal talent.' Sunday Times.

Running Dream by **Trish Cooke**, tells the story of three generations of West Indian women with warmth and humour.
'the author's promise ripens.' The Times.

Song for a Sanctuary by **Rukhsana Ahmad,** explores the painful dilemma of an Asian woman forced to seek help from a woman's refuge.   'perceptive and moving.' Morning Star.

Leonora's Dance by **Zindika**, four women share the house of a black ballet dancer, whose contact with the supernatural lays the ghosts of the past to rest.   'a compelling show.' Caribbean Times.

Monsoon by **Maya Chowdhry,** is a poetic account of a young woman's sexual awakening.
'evocative and sensual.' Radio Times.

A Hero's Welcome by **Winsome Pinnock**, a tale of misplaced loyalty, longing for escape and early love.
'terrific new play' The Independent.

'showcases a wealth of talent amongst Black and Asian communities ...often neglected by mainstream publishers.' Black Pride Magazine

Price: £7.50   **ISBN 0-9515877-2-2**

SEVEN PLAYS BY WOMEN: Female Voices, Fighting Lives
ed. Cheryl Robson

A bumper collection of award-winning plays by a new generation of women writers together with short critical essays on theatre today.

Fail/Safe by **Ayshe Raif,** 'a most disturbing lament for the way that some family ties become chains from which there will never be escape...' The Guardian

The Taking of Liberty by **Cheryl Robson,** 'the extraordinary tale of a town in the French Revolution: when the women take offence at an improvised statue, the incident escalates into savage retribution.' What's On.

Crux by **April de Angelis**, follows four women who follow their own doctrine of pleasure and hedonism in opposition to the stifling dictates of the Church. 'stimulating and humorous new play.' Time Out.

Ithaka by **Nina Rapi,** 'theatrically inventive, often surreal, witty and funny....sensitive charting of a woman's quest for love and freedom.' Bush Theatre.

Cochon Flambé by **Eva Lewin,** explores the sexual politics of waitressing in a comic, one-woman play.

Cut it Out by **Jan Ruppe**, a sharp blend of humour and pathos, tells the story of Laura, a self-lacerator.

Forced Out by **Jean Abbott**, a powerful drama of a lesbian teacher's confrontation with her community's prejudices, unleashed by a newspaper's gay witchhunt.

'a testimony to the work and debate that is going on among women, artistically, theoretically and practically. It is an inspiring document.' What's On

Price: £5.95   **ISBN: 0-9515877-1-4**

THE WOMEN WRITERS' HANDBOOK
eds: Robson, Georgeson, Beck

An essential guide to setting up and running your own writing workshops.

Creative Writing Exercises

Extracts from workshop writings-
new poetry and fiction

Contact Directory

Essays on writing and dramaturgy by

CARYL CHURCHILL
JILL HYEM
BRYONY LAVERY
AYSHE RAIF
CHERYL ROBSON

A gem of a book. Everything a woman writer might need in one slim volume. Everywoman Magazine

PRICE:£4.95   **ISBN: 0-9515877-0-6**

HOW MAXINE LEARNED TO LOVE HER LEGS
and other tales of growing-up
ed: Sarah Le Fanu

A sparkling collection of short stories exploring a host of female parts - rites of passage, revelations, strange relationships, love, loss, danger - the pleasures and pains of growing up female in one entertaining volume.

Featuring 23 new and established authors including:

HILARY BAILEY
BONNIE GREER
KIRSTY GUNN
GERALDINE KAYE
KATE PULLINGER
RAVI RANDHAWA
MICHELE ROBERTS
ELISA SEGRAVE

'Being a clerical officer wasn't a bad job but April was a girl, who at 12 years of age had reupholstered a 3-piece suite without a pattern.'

'she only went to school to please her mum, because looking after mum was the most important thing... she felt more like her mum was her and she was her mum. A pity they couldn't swap.'

'Auntie Poonam always thought things were worse when done in broad daylight...in front of the whole world, sister. Shameless!'

'I have a young erotic mother...'

PRICE: £8.95   **ISBN: 0-9515877-4-9**